T0318384

Cambridge Elements ≡

Elements in the Problems of God
edited by
Michael L. Peterson
Asbury Theological Seminary

DIVINE GUIDANCE

Moral Attraction in Action

Paul K. Moser
Loyola University Chicago

CAMBRIDGE
UNIVERSITY PRESS

Shaftesbury Road, Cambridge CB2 8EA, United Kingdom

One Liberty Plaza, 20th Floor, New York, NY 10006, USA

477 Williamstown Road, Port Melbourne, VIC 3207, Australia

314–321, 3rd Floor, Plot 3, Splendor Forum, Jasola District Centre, New Delhi – 110025, India

103 Penang Road, #05–06/07, Visioncrest Commercial, Singapore 238467

Cambridge University Press is part of Cambridge University Press & Assessment, a department of the University of Cambridge.

We share the University's mission to contribute to society through the pursuit of education, learning and research at the highest international levels of excellence.

www.cambridge.org
Information on this title: www.cambridge.org/9781009269704

DOI: 10.1017/9781009269698

First published 2022

A catalogue record for this publication is available from the British Library.

ISBN 978-1-009-26970-4 Paperback
ISSN 2754-8724 (online)
ISSN 2754-8716 (print)

Divine Guidance

Moral Attraction in Action

Elements in the Problems of God

DOI: 10.1017/9781009269698
First published online: September 2022

Paul K. Moser
Loyola University Chicago
Author for correspondence: Paul K. Moser, pmoser@luc.edu

Abstract: If God exists and is perfectly good, God tries to guide people. A twofold question then arises: How does God (try to) guide people, and to what end? Problems of divine guidance for humans, according to this volume, are real and serious, but they are manageable once we clarify the kind of God at issue. According to the volume's main thesis, if God has a perfect moral character accompanied by certain redemptive purposes for humans, the puzzling nature of divine guidance for them need not preclude the reality of such guidance. It is, this volume contends, a live option for God to guide or lead humans toward goodness, even if the leading is not fully explainable by humans. The voluntary moral attraction of cooperative humans by divine goodness is central to divine guidance, and it can illuminate the kind of evidence to be expected from God.

Keywords: divine guidance, moral attraction, evidence of God, suffering and evil, divine goodness

ISBNs: 9781009269704 (PB), 9781009269698 (OC)
ISSNs: 2754-8724 (online), 2754-8716 (print)

Contents

1 Guides Galore

He guides me in paths of righteousness for his name's sake. —Psalm 23:3

If God exists and is perfectly good, God tries to guide people. In that case, a twofold question arises: *How* does God (try to) guide people, and *to what end*? Problems of divine guidance for humans, according to this volume, are real and serious, but they are manageable for them, at least in principle. This claim depends on the kind of God at issue. According to the volume's main thesis, if God has a perfectly good moral character accompanied by certain redemptive purposes for humans, the puzzling nature of divine guidance for them need not preclude the reality of such guidance. It is, this volume contends, a live option for God to guide or lead humans toward goodness, even if the leading is not fully explainable by humans. The voluntary moral attraction of cooperative humans by divine goodness, we shall see, is central to divine guidance.

We shall consider the apostle Paul at times as an exemplary candidate for receiving and illuminating divine guidance. He offers the following remark to indicate the importance of such guidance: "All who are led by the Spirit of God are children of God" (Rom. 8:14). Paul had in mind, we shall see, divine leading that relies on self-manifested divine goodness that is attractive toward humans and yields a distinctive kind of evidence of God in human moral experience. This is leading by the intentional, goal-directed power of God's moral character, including divine righteous love and jealousy. Such leading can rely on divine representation in human conscience. This is divine leading by God's moral attracting of cooperative people; it attracts them to cooperate by divine moral power, without coercing them. So, we must attend to God's moral character, with regard to its righteous love and jealousy, to understand divine guidance. This perspective will clarify how divine guiding contributes to our understanding of evidence of God's reality and goodness. (My use of some of Paul's letters and some other Biblical writings has its basis in what best explains our relevant experiences as evidence, and not in any sweeping view of Biblical authority.)

Basic Guiding

We should distinguish between basic and nonbasic guiding. *Basic guiding* from God arises as a requirement of divine righteousness: God would not be righteous in failing to offer it, and humans would violate divine righteousness in failing to cooperate with it. God's general aim to lead people in righteousness as moral goodness anchors basic guidance. So, if God refused to offer any cooperative people guidance toward treating other people with unselfish care rather than hate, God would not be righteous. In addition, if God offered such guidance and we humans went against it, we would not be righteous. Even if we are unclear about what is righteous or morally good in some cases, other cases are clear to us. For instance, our neglect of needy refugee children whom we can easily help is morally bad, regardless of any contrary social custom in our society.

Nonbasic guiding is found in cases where our departure from divine leadership does not entail our being unrighteous. For instance, if God guides ancient Israel not to eat shellfish (Lev. 11:9, Deut. 14:9), for whatever reason, their eating shellfish does not entail their being unrighteous; nor does God's lifting a ban on their eating shellfish entail divine unrighteousness. So, not all divine guiding is basic in the sense indicated. God can give guidance for purposes other than insuring the righteousness of its recipients. We shall focus, however, on basic guiding and its intended righteousness because such guiding reveals God's moral character and our moral responsibility in reply.

Basic guiding can be either successful or unsuccessful regarding righteousness because human cooperation can be either present or absent in response to it. For example, King Ahab in ancient Israel (ca. 860 BCE) chose to go against God's guiding him as ruler of Israel:

> Ahab son of Omri did evil in the sight of the Lord more than all who were before him. And as if it had been a light thing for him to walk in the sins of Jeroboam son of Nebat, he took as his wife Jezebel daughter of King Ethbaal of the Sidonians, and went and served Baal, and worshiped him. He erected an altar for Baal in the house of Baal, which he built in Samaria. Ahab also made a sacred pole. Ahab did more to provoke the anger of the Lord, the God of Israel, than had all the kings of Israel who were before him (1 Kings 16:30–33, NRSV here and in subsequent Biblical translations, unless otherwise noted).

God's attempt to guide humans, then, can fail in relation to an individual human or to a group of humans. This can prompt divine anger and even judgment. (Section 2 returns to the latter topic.)

Paul, unlike king Ahab, chose to obey God's basic guiding for the sake of cooperating with God. He did not have the political responsibility to lead Israel as its King, but he had an equally important, if broader, charge: to bring God's good news of righteous redemption to the Gentiles. This was in accordance with his understanding of the book of Isaiah, as we shall see.

Which Guide, Whose God?

Concepts of God are legion, for better or worse. A quick sample corresponds to the international roster of deities: Shiva, Vishnu, Krishna, Baal, Marduk, Ashur, Asherah, El, YHWH, Zeus, Athena, Thor. The list goes on, well beyond the big names. An urgent problem for our inquiry is: Where to begin? Some people choose not to begin because progress toward credible answers in favor of God seems hopeless to them. The historical and interpretive data are complex and elusive in a way that threatens proposed evidence favoring God, or at least the responsible handling of it.

Some concepts of God are, by a standard of moral decency, more attractive than others. ISIS, for instance, wields a notion of God that promotes human beheading and rape, leaving us with a God who merits moral censure. Similarly, Osama bin Laden and other al-Qaeda leaders have claimed that their violent activities, including their destruction of New York's Twin Towers on September 11, 2001, are motivated by "the cause of God." In the same vein, many pro-Trump insurrectionists against the election of US President Joe Biden have claimed that God told them to invade the US Capitol on January 6, 2021, bent on violence. We should not take such claims to be guided by God at face value, however, if God is worthy of human worship and trust. They raise serious ethical questions about the character of a God who would guide humans with such immoral efforts.

Human history leaves us with a need to sift for a worthy God in a mixed pool of candidates. We should send all candidates, including various Biblical candidates, through a conceptual sieve involving moral righteousness appropriate to a God who merits worship. We thus will have a demanding but illuminating starting place for sifting by setting the conceptual bar for God high, indeed as high as possible: God as *worthy of worship* and thus morally perfect in righteousness.

We shall assume that worthiness of worship requires being worthy of full adoration, trust, and commitment, and that moral perfection requires freedom from any moral deficiency regarding moral goodness, rightness, or praise-worthiness. We can allow for some disagreement over the conditions for moral perfection and worthiness of worship, as long as a common core of conditions is in place. Grey areas in concepts among inquirers do not exclude such a common core, and this holds for a range of general normative concepts. The relevant concepts still have significant contours for guiding inquiry and action, as we shall see in the case of moral perfection in righteousness.

Our conceptual starting place, in the notion of worthiness of worship, will discourage us from settling for lesser gods, such as gods of our own making or gods for our own convenience. We thus can exclude, at the start, gods given to selfish opportunism of the kind familiar among humans. Whether any god will survive our needed assessment remains to be seen. Our notion of God, however, should be morally in order, regardless of whether it is satisfied by an actual titleholder for the term "God." A title, such as "the present king of Canada," can be intelligible even if no one actually satisfies it. This holds, too, for the perfectionist title "God."

Our question now is: What is it like to be worthy of worship and thus morally perfect? We can pursue this question even if God does not exist. The question becomes, in its cautious interpretation: What *would* it be like to be God in relation to humans and their experience, *if* a God worthy of worship exists. A quick answer states that it is, or would be, very different from what it is like to be an ordinary human in relation to other humans. Moral character is a major area of contrast. God has, or at least would have, perfection (and hence no deficiency) in that area, but ordinary humans do not. Universal human agreement rarely emerges in any area, but it seems to apply to the truth that ordinary humans are morally imperfect to some extent.

God would differ from humans in many areas, such as the areas of relative power, knowledge, and control. We will focus, however, on the area of moral difference, particularly regarding moral goodness and guidance. The latter twofold area is particularly illuminating because it figures centrally in worthiness of worship, and it offers a definite contrast between God and typical humans. This area bears on pertinent evidence for God's reality and presence, as we shall see, even though the latter consideration is often neglected by inquirers. In attacking theology, H. L. Mencken remarked: "I have paid relatively little attention to the ethical aspect of religion, for I am convinced that that aspect is largely fortuitous" (1930: viii). This is a serious mistake, however, because the very notion of God as worthy of worship requires being moral perfect.

A God worthy of worship would aim to guide willing people toward having a good society. So, this question arises: What would it be like to be a God worthy of worship who seeks to guide humans uncoercively to inhabit and promote a society, or kingdom, reflective of perfect moral goodness? Our attention to this question will highlight the character and the main purpose of a God worthy of worship. This approach will enable us to discern the presence or absence of God in human experience. We need, however, to consider the responsibility of inquirers in their asking about God and divine guidance.

Inquirers under Question

When people ask about God, we can inquire about their attitudes and motives. Who is asking about God, and why are they (or we) asking? Why do they care, for instance, about our question of what it would be like to be God in relation to humans and their experience? Perhaps there is genuine value in knowing a correct answer, and inquirers can seek that value. For instance, some inquirers may desire to identify and to share God's power and main purpose for the good of all concerned. Others may settle, however, for improved understanding of the world as a result of God's superior understanding, even if they are indifferent about improving themselves or society.

We should expect God to care about inquirers' attitudes regarding God, for their own good, because those attitudes matter, morally, interpersonally, and otherwise. If people seek a correct answer to our question about God for a purpose at odds with God's purpose, a problem may arise. God reasonably could frustrate their effort, perhaps by hiding divine self-manifestation and related evidence of God from them, at least for a time. God then may postpone self-manifestation to them until they are ready to share God's main purpose for the good of all concerned (see Moser [2020, chapters 7 and 8] and Moser [2021a]). So, the self-examination of inquirers is fitting. They need to ask if they themselves are interfering somehow with available evidence of God from divine self-manifestation. Such interfering is a live option for inquirers about God, even if widely neglected among theists, agnostics, and atheists.

God would need somehow to reveal the main divine purpose to inquirers, given that they cannot discover it on their own. Even so, nothing in principle precludes God's revealing that purpose to them and guiding them in sharing it under suitable conditions. Do we have any indication in experience of such revealing and guiding? If we do not, the case for God's reality and goodness will be difficult indeed. Agnosticism then will be a live option. So, what is available in human experience will bear importantly on our assessment of divine reality and guidance.

However we specify our preferred concept of God, people who believe in God as a redeemer of humans share a common commitment. They assume that God guides, or leads, people at times, as a function of God's being their authoritative "Lord." They hold that divine lordship includes divine leadership of a morally important kind. This consideration returns us to an issue suggested above: how to identify, at least in principle, morally acceptable divine guidance? Not just any leading alleged to come from God will count, if God is morally good. So, we must separate the wheat from the chaff in the field of claimants to divine leadership. We thus need a moral filter to separate divine guidance from the many counterfeits in the area.

This volume aims to illuminate divine guidance via a notion of God as *worthy* of worship and thus morally perfect, without begging the question of God's existence. The most prominent Biblical conception of God, from Abraham to Isaiah to Jesus to Paul, portrays God as righteous without defect, and this volume recruits this theme to separate fake divine guidance from the real item. As a result, we need to attend, with discernment, to some Biblical testimony about God's character. Despite some disagreements about perfect righteousness, people can have genuine moral knowledge that, for instance, the terror of ISIS is morally bad, or that care for refugees in desperate need is morally good. The volume outlines how such optimism about moral knowledge endures.

The topic of divine guidance is complicated by a problem of divine elusiveness, including people being left without supporting evidence for guidance that they can control or reproduce. Contrary to Martin Buber, we shall see, the Biblical God does not "remain present" to the awareness of people, including faithful people. Instead, this God hides from people at times, leaving them without definite guidance. Pascal (1658) observed that a religion failing to acknowledge this problem is false. He was right. Even so, not all is lost for divine guidance; it can proceed with due subtlety, as this volume explains.

God, we shall see, could use divine elusiveness, including an absence of guidance at times, to challenge people toward deeper righteousness. A contrast between divine presence and its absence can awaken appreciation of such presence, but the matter is not unilateral. God would expect human responsiveness through cooperation. This would enable divine presence and guidance to reach their intended fruition in divine power humanly received for unselfish social good. Divine guidance, then, is not a monologue; it relies on interpersonal efforts that humans can frustrate. So, divine success in guidance is not guaranteed. It would be rejectable by humans who do not want or allow it, including humans who find it offensive to human autonomy or maturity. We also shall see that God could seek to guide humans without their recognizing this effort. This volume explains how God would seek success in divine guidance, via moral attraction coupled with human cooperation.

God as Guiding Ruler

A distinctive theme of ancient Judaism is that God *rules*, even prior to the origin of the Jewish monarchy with King Saul. An early sign of this ruling arises with Jerubbaal (aka Gideon): "Then the Israelites said to Gideon, 'Rule over us, you and your son and your grandson also; for you have delivered us out of the hand of Midian.' Gideon said to them, 'I will not rule over you, and my son will not rule over you; the Lord will rule over [אֶמְשֹׁל; *'emšōl*] you'" (Judges 8:22–23). A similar testimony to God reigning as king comes from "the Song of Moses" before the monarchy: "The Lord will reign [יִמְלֹךְ; *yimlōk*] forever and ever" (Exodus 15:18). We need to clarify such kingly rule for God, in order to understand divine guidance.

The story of Samuel, like the story of Gideon, assumes divine kingship prior to the Jewish monarchy: "The Lord said to Samuel, 'Listen to the voice of the people in all that they say to you; for they have not rejected you, but they have rejected me from being king [מִמְּלֹךְ; *mimməlōk*] over them'" (1 Sam. 8:7). Similarly, having arranged for Saul to be King over Israel, Samuel remarks: "When you saw that King Nahash of the Ammonites came against you, you said to me, 'No, but a king shall reign over us,' though the Lord your God was your king [מַלְכְּכֶם; *malkəkem*]" (1 Sam. 12:12; cf. DSS 4Q51 Samuel A). (Samuel has in mind a time before the installment of Saul as king.)

The previous passages assume that God is ruler-king over the Israelites, despite the absence of a human king in Israel. They thus assume that divine kingship can be direct in not depending on human kingship. They allow for a direct kingly role for divine guidance, without reliance on human royal authority of the kind found in many theocracies supervised by humans. Divine kingship in ancient Israel includes God as guiding ruler, sometimes without human supervision. Ancient Israel combines divine lordship and kingship in one God, with or without a subsidiary human king. So, divine kingship for ancient Israel can proceed without a monarchy or theocracy supervised by humans. This is important because it allows Israel's God to be more than a national God, to be a kingly God even in the absence of human kingship. We shall explore some important consequences of this consideration for divine guidance.

Martin Buber, following H. J. Kraus, has summed up the role of God as ruler in ancient Israel as follows: "Israel – this means 'May God manifest Himself as Lord, Ruler!' This is what it comes to: the realization of the all-embracing rulership of God is the Proton and Eschaton of Israel" (1967: 58). Buber adds:

> YHWH is indeed a *melek*, but He transcends the nature of a Semitic *malk*-god so intrinsically that a formula must be avoided which could threaten to want to restrict Him to it . . . . That which I regard . . . as the central [idea] among the ancient religious ideas of Israel is something which emerges from early texts; it can be expressed in the words: *YHWH leads us* . . . . YHWH [is] revered and trusted as *the God who leads the community* . . . . This divine Lord . . . leads his own Himself, directly, as a sheik leads his wandering tribe (1967: 22–23).

We need to clarify the relevant idea of divine ruling as direct *leading* if we are to understand divine kingship. Our clarification will contrast with A. N. Whitehead's characterization of ancient Jewish monotheism: "The early, naive trend of Semitic monotheism, Jewish and Mahometan, is towards the notion of Law imposed by the fiat of the One God" (1933: 125). We shall identify an alternative to Whitehead's suggestion of "Law imposed." The relevant divine leading, we shall see, takes a different, uncoercive form neglected by many inquirers.

Guiding toward Goodness

The God of ancient Israel has and promotes righteousness, including morally perfect goodness, aimed at human salvation that transcends national boundaries. This righteousness includes steadfast love, faithfulness, and justice based on such goodness, including in interpersonal relationships. Some of the Jewish Psalms give a central place to this righteousness. For instance:

> The Lord is king! Let the earth rejoice;
> let the many coastlands be glad!
> Clouds and thick darkness are all around him;
> righteousness [צֶדֶק; *ṣedeq*] and justice are the foundation of his throne . . . .
> For you, O Lord, are most high over all the earth;
> you are exalted far above all gods (Psalm 97:1–2, 9).

Psalm 89 endorses God's kingly righteousness:

> Righteousness and justice are the foundation of your throne;
> steadfast love and faithfulness go before you.
> Happy are the people who know the festal shout,
> who walk, O Lord, in the light of your countenance;
> they exult in your name all day long,
> and extol your righteousness (Psalm 89:14–16).

The righteous God of Israel, according to Jeremiah, will raise up a human king devoted to divine righteousness and thereby to the salvation of God's people: "The days are surely coming, says the Lord, when I will raise up for David a righteous Branch, and he shall reign as king and deal wisely, and shall execute justice and righteousness in the land. In his days Judah will be saved [תִּוָּשַׁע; *tiwwāšaʻ*] and Israel will live in safety. And this is the name by which he will be called: 'The Lord is our righteousness'" (Jer. 23:5–6; cf. Jer. 9:23–24). Divine righteousness, according to Jeremiah, will result in Judah's being "saved."

The book of Isaiah links divine righteousness to salvation among humans:

> I form light and create darkness,
> I make weal and create woe [רָע; *rāʻ*];
> I the Lord do all these things.
> Shower, O heavens, from above,
> and let the skies rain down righteousness;
> let the earth open, that salvation [יֶשַׁע; *yešaʻ*] may spring up,
> and let it cause righteousness to sprout up also;
> I the Lord have created it. (Isa. 45:6–8; cf. Isa. 59:15–17)

According to the book of Isaiah, God creates conflict (not to be confused with evil) in order to bring righteousness to people, and that righteousness seeks salvation for them. Psalm 74 connects divine kingship and salvation for people: "God my King is from of old, working salvation in the earth" (Psalm 74:12). Ancient Judaism thus relates divine kingship to divine and human righteousness and thereby to human salvation by God. We need to clarify that relation to illuminate divine guidance.

The God of ancient Israel functions as an Über-King and an Über-God: a King over all other kings, and a God over all other gods (Psalm 82). This "over-relation" is presented as having rightful authority, with the God of Israel as the worthy top authority over all other kings and gods. After announcing that "the Lord is King," as cited above, Psalm 97 states: "For you, O Lord, are most high [עֶלְיוֹן; *elyōn*] over all the earth; you are exalted far above all gods" (Psalm 97:9). Psalm 82, as noted, makes all other gods in the pantheon subsidiary to the "Most High" God of Israel: "I say, 'You are gods, children of the Most High [עֶלְיוֹן], all of you'" (Psalm 82:6). Israel's righteous God is thus the Über-God and therefore an Über-King over all other powers, in heaven and on earth. (On Israel's notion of the "Most High" God in connection with El and related divine figures, see Smith [2001: 47–53]; cf. Mettinger [1988: 95, 122]. On the role of Psalm 82 as defining God in terms of righteousness, see Moberly [2020: 93–123].)

An important question concerns the nature of the superior power characteristic of Israel's "Most High" God and King. The struggle in ancient Israel to identify and represent that power includes a conflict over who God really is, in contrast with lesser or false gods. That conflict has not disappeared in subsequent inquiry, particularly when issues of divine righteousness and guidance arise.

The book of Deuteronomy ascribes universal authority to its "Most High" God: "When the Most High apportioned the nations, when he divided human-kind, he fixed the boundaries of the peoples according to the number of the gods; the Lord's own portion was his people, Jacob his allotted share" (Deut. 32:8–9). Israel thus has a special relation to the "Most High" God, but this is not an exclusive relation toward other nations. (See Mikva [2020: 103–19].) This God works across national boundaries to promote divine righteousness and salvation (Isa. 25:6–8, Amos 9:11–12, Micah 7:16–17), even though Israel has a special redemptive purpose. We need to examine this transnational divine work.

From Guiding to Hiding

Divine guiding in ancient Israel attracted conflicting responses and interpretations. Commenting on YHWH as "the One-who-goes-on-before," Buber has identified some variations: "The leading of the One-who-goes-on-before remained so much the central idea of Israelitish faith that the wilderness-wandering reported by the narrator as the punishment of an entire generation of people and also remembered as such in song (Psalm 95:10ff.), appeared to many singers and story-tellers as an abundant mercy [cf. Psalm 136:13–16, Jer. 2:6]" (1967: 102). According to Buber, "YHWH is the One who is with them, the One who remains present to them, thus the One who comes-along with them (Ex. 13:21, Num. 14:14, Deut. 1:30, 33), the Leader, the *melek*" (1967: 104). (Buber approved the English translation of the body of his book.) On this basis, Buber ascribes to God the view that "you do not need to conjure me, but you cannot conjure me either." He thus endorses the "de-magicizing" of faith in this God (1967: 106).

Buber points to a central role for the divine leading of humans from God's kingship, but the divine role in ancient Israel is more complicated than he suggests. God's "remaining present" to the people in ancient Israel is not as continuous as Buber suggests. The recurring themes in the Jewish Bible of divine self-hiding and of the human need to seek God confirm the complexity of the matter. The theme of divine self-hiding of God's presence from humans arises repeatedly in the Jewish Bible. For instance: "Truly, you are a God who hides himself, O God of Israel, the Savior" (Isa. 45:15). Similarly, the psalmist asks God: "Why do you hide your face? Why do you forget our affliction and oppression?" (Psalm 44:24). These remarks assume that God does not constantly "remain present" to the awareness of the people of Israel. Indeed, they assume that God actively self-hides from people on occasion. (See McEntire [2013] and Terrien [1978]. Buber [1952] takes exception to talk of God as "hidden.")

The Biblical theme of a human need to seek God fits with the theme of divine self-hiding on occasion. An example comes from Jeremiah: "When you search for me, you will find me; if you seek me with all your heart, I will let you find me, says the Lord" (Jer. 29:13–14). A second example arises in Deuteronomy: "From there you will seek the Lord your God, and you will find him if you search after him with all your heart and soul" (Deut. 4:29). There would be no need for searching after God if God constantly "remained present" to the (awareness of the) people of Israel. According to the Jewish Bible, God is often elusive and calls for human searching after God. Buber's account of divine kingly leadership neglects this important consideration. So, we need an approach to divine kingship and guidance that corrects this neglect.

According to the Jewish Bible, God worked among, and was present to, people outside ancient Israel for various divine purposes, even if the people of

Israel were unaware of this at the time. Cyrus the Great of Persia serves as an example of such divine work, in second Isaiah:

> Thus says the Lord to his anointed, to Cyrus,
> whose right hand I have grasped
> to subdue nations before him
> and strip kings of their robes,
> to open doors before him –
> and the gates shall not be closed:
> I will go before you
> and level the mountains,
> I will break in pieces the doors of bronze
> and cut through the bars of iron
> (Isa. 45:1–2; cf. Isa. 41:2–25, 42:6).

On a more positive note: "In the first year of King Cyrus of Persia, in fulfillment of the word of the Lord spoken by Jeremiah, the Lord stirred up the spirit of King Cyrus of Persia so that he sent a herald throughout all his kingdom and also declared in a written edict: 'Thus says King Cyrus of Persia: The Lord, the God of heaven, has given me all the kingdoms of the earth, and he has charged me to build him a house at Jerusalem, which is in Judah'" (2 Chron. 36:22–23). According to the Jewish Bible, then, ancient Israel was not the only recipient of divine leading. Such leading, in addition, occurred even when it was not recognized to be divine by those who were led by God (Isa. 42:16).

The divine leading of humans toward a righteous community does not always rely on a recognized human authority in a political theocracy. *The Oxford English Dictionary, 3d ed.,* offers the following on "theocracy": "A form of government in which God (or a deity) is recognized as the king or immediate ruler, and his laws are taken as the statute-book of the kingdom, these laws being usually administered by a priestly order as his ministers and agents; hence (loosely) a system of government by a sacerdotal order, claiming a divine commission; also, a state so governed: especially applied to the commonwealth of Israel from the exodus to the election of Saul as king." Saul's kingship did represent a recognized political theocracy, but the role of divine kingship in ancient Israel was not always so explicit as a social structure.

Buber has noted how theocracy can be externally minimalist in ancient Israel: "There is in pre-kingly Israel no externality of rulership; for there is no political sphere except the theopolitical, and all sons of Israel are directly related to YHWH, who chooses and rejects, gives an order and withdraws it" (1967: 136). Buber observes how YHWH typically allows for freedom in human responses to divine challenges and expectations, in conjunction with a divine desire for a righteous community. Divine coercion of human wills toward God is not the main motivator in divine leadership. The "direct" theocracy noted by Buber proceeds without a royal political system, let alone a coercive system, of human rulers, despite the subsidiary guiding role of priests and prophets. Only God is king as ruler of Israel prior to Saul, and when a human king is introduced later, God remains as Über-King, to whom all people, even approved political leaders, are accountable.

Divine leadership without an explicit public structure typically will create turbulence and frustration for humans, particularly for group decision-making and action. A person then can lack direct evidence of the divine leading had by another person or a group of other persons, with no recourse to a publicly shared standard for a resolution. In addition, the divine intervention in a human life for the sake of moral leading would not need human preparation or permission. It could come as a surprise and start a new, deeper variation on righteousness among humans. Such change can be socially disruptive, as the history of ancient Israel shows. The leading of its God can create social turbulence for the sake of rightening, or rectifying, wayward human relationships toward righteousness. We need to consider a distinctive social aim in the divine turbulence in guidance toward righteousness.

Guiding for Family Provision

The God of ancient Israel aims, sometimes with surprises, to lead people (deeper) into a righteous relationship with God and others. Two of many obvious cases are the laughable promise of a child to the aged Abraham and Sarah (Gen. 18:10–15) and the breathtaking divine challenge to Abraham to sacrifice Isaac (Gen. 22:1–18). The God of ancient Israel thus exceeds the expectations of humans, whether they are inside or outside Israel. Redemptive surprise is often the result of divine guidance.

The God of ancient Israel is not *altogether* ineffable, incomprehensible, or inscrutable. Some definite attributions do apply, and *must* apply, to a God worthy of worship and trust: attributions concerning righteousness, faithfulness, mercy, and so on. Divine righteousness, however, would be more profound than our own righteousness, and thus would go beyond our specific expectations for God at times. Divine redemptive surprise, then, would be a live option for humans relative to God. By way of a striking example, some interpreters, perhaps including Jesus, would cite the role of an approved messiah from God who suffers and dies to attract people to God (see Moser [2021b: chapter 5]). This would exceed ordinary human expectations, inside or outside Israel.

A direct theocracy without human supervision allows for divine redemptive surprise of humans. The surprise would be redemptive owing to its intention to bring good out of bad for humans. It allows for God to be an Über-King who rightly has and exercises authority over any human group of leaders, including kings and priests. In that case, human leaders are limited and subsidiary in their authority in a way that leaves room for divine authority and a deeper divine righteousness, even with surprises.

Contrary to Kierkegaard's pseudonymous *Fear and Trembling* (1843), we should not expect God to suspend or to transcend morality or righteousness, unless we are willing to end up with God as demonic, as Buber has observed (1952: 113–20). Instead, we should expect divine righteousness to be shown to be more profound than we humans initially expect and to try to lead us deeper into such righteousness, for the sake of the common good. A group of human political authorities who block this option, even while claiming to uphold a theocracy, would be antithetical to the movement of divine redemption in righteousness.

A theocracy with human supervision should be avowedly subsidiary in representing God. It thus should be open to corrective revision in the subsidiary and fallible authority assigned to its human leaders. It is well-advised to acknowledge divine corrective authority over any human representatives and traditions, thereby allowing for moral deepening prompted by new manifestations of divine righteousness. Human "infallibility," whether in a group or in an individual, does not fit with this approach to a righteous Über-God. Such infallibility would tread on the authority that belongs only to the kingly Über-God (cf. Isa. 44:6–8).

The approach to divine kingship and guidance on offer safeguards what we may call the "mystery" of a perfectly good God. Terence Fretheim has remarked: "Both God and Moses recognize that God is not demystified through further understanding. In fact, the more one understands God, the more mysterious God becomes. God is the supreme exemplification of the old adage: The more you know, the more you know you don't know" (1991: 62–63). R. W. L. Moberly adds that "the recognition of God as a mystery aligns well with the bush that burns without being destroyed, the bush whose unconsuming fire is alive and not on a trajectory towards death" (2020: 79). (Moberly finds the same kind of mystery suggested by the use of "YHWH" in the Jewish scriptures.) Such openness to a righteous Über-God who exceeds our full understanding and expectation can save humans from abuse by human systems of authority, including political authority.

The divine mystery in ancient Israel includes divine elusiveness for humans, and this can complicate human testing for divine reality and guidance. Such elusiveness, however, can lead willing people to a new depth of seriousness about divine righteousness, given their experience of divine absence. We do not need to have (nor do we have) a full theodicy of explaining God's ways to appreciate this lesson, as Section 3 contends. Divine reasons for self-hiding at a time can, and often do, elude us, just as such reasons for allowing evil can and often do. We should expect this of a transcendent God who works with relatively limited humans in order to promote righteousness that exceeds their expectations. (Sections 3 and 4 will return to the complexity of testing for divine reality and guidance.)

At times, ancient Israel faced the mystery of their kingly God by combining their understanding of God as Über-king with an understanding of God as divine father. Psalm 89 affirms this combination by addressing God as enthroned king: "Righteousness and justice are the foundation of your throne [כִּסְאֶךָ; *kis-'e-ḵā*]," and then portraying God to say: "He [the Davidic king of Israel] shall cry to me, 'You are my Father [אָבִי; *'ā-ḇî*], my God, and the Rock of my salvation'" (Psalm 89:14, 26). It thus would be misleading to suggest that calling to God as "my Father" is unique to Jesus and foreign to the Jewish Bible (see Jeremias [1967: 29]). At least it is unclear that Psalm 89 offers only a "corporate, national, or covenantal sense" of "Father" (Fitzmyer [1981: vol. 2, 903]). Psalm 89 allows that divine fatherhood applies to Israel via the Davidic king, but this, of course, does not preclude divine fatherhood for individual members of Israel.

In the Gospel of Luke, Jesus ascribes to God a combination of divine kingship and fatherhood reminiscent of Psalm 89: "Do not be afraid, little flock, for it is your Father's good pleasure to give you the kingdom" (Luke 12:32). Similarly, in the Lord's Prayer, God is "Father" who has a "kingdom" (Luke 11:2; Matt. 6:9–10). In addition, this prayer from Jesus shows a concern for divine leading: leading away from a time of failure in trial (Luke 11:4; Matt. 6:13).

God as Father has beloved children, according to Jesus, and thus is a family leader committed to family provision for the children. This provision has a moral focus, as indicated by a remark attributed to Jesus by Matthew's Gospel: "I say to you, Love your enemies and pray for those who persecute you, so that you may be children of your Father in heaven .... Be perfect, therefore, as your heavenly Father is perfect" (Matt. 5:44–45, 48; cf. Luke 6:35–36). Indeed, Jesus understands the filial relation to God in terms of doing God's will: "Whoever does the will of God is my brother and sister and mother" (Mark 3:35). This volitional understanding is confirmed by Jesus's prayer to God in Gethsemane: "Abba, Father, for you all things are possible; remove this cup from me; yet, not what I want, but what you want" (Mark 14:36). God's fatherly role is thus inherently moral, requiring obedience to God, and such obedience is expected of God's family, inside and outside Israel.

The moral center of divine guidance rests on a normative standard of "Like father, like child," in matters of moral character, and thus "Like Father, like family," again in matters of moral character. The standard emerges early in ancient Israel: "You shall be holy, for I the Lord your God am holy" (Lev. 19:2; cf. 1 Pet. 1:16), with holiness requiring righteousness as moral goodness. This standard concerns how humans should *be*, morally, not just how they should behave. So, it goes deeper than action, and thus raises the question of how humans can *become* righteous in relation to divine guidance. (Section 3 returns to that question.)

The desired family of the divine father is no ordinary family. Its moral core in divine righteousness transcends physical lineage, and it focuses on human willing in relation to God's moral character. As a result, such a role for family is a matter of divine family renovation toward human families, challenging any exclusive national, ethnic, and racial boundaries that block family membership. This consideration underlies the mission of Paul toward the Gentiles as part of God's "family of faith" (Gal. 6:10), in contrast with a family of physical origins. (See Dunn [2003: 592–99].)

If God seeks to be the father of a global kingdom family, this effort will bear on divine guidance. We turn to how moral filial possession figures in this guided quest for a kingdom family.

2 Guiding with a Vengeance

> You shall worship no other god, because the Lord, whose name is Jealous, is a jealous God. – Exodus 34:14

Divine guidance in ancient Israel has unexpected motives, such as divine jealousy and vengeance. We need to ask if they are virtuous rather than vicious. Some illumination comes from clarification of a divine goal of personal and social renovation in the leading of humans.

Toward a Kingdom Family

The evidence in the Jewish Bible regarding God's moral character and resulting guidance of humans is inconsistent. Some Biblical claims lower God to the immoral level of hateful humans. For instance, Psalm 5 says of God: "You hate all evildoers ... . The Lord abhors the bloodthirsty and deceitful" (Psalm 5:5–6). Psalm 11 reiterates: "The Lord ... hates the lover of violence" (Psalm 11:5–6). It is doubtful that such characterizations are consistent with the Biblical command, attributed to God, to love neighbors: "You shall love your neighbor as yourself: I am the Lord" (Lev. 19:18). The present defect arises from characterizing God in a familiar human image of immoral animus toward one's enemies.

When we add some New Testament evidence to the mix, inconsistency across various Biblical portraits of God becomes clear. In Matthew's Gospel, for instance, Jesus commands: "You have heard that it was said, 'You shall love your neighbor and hate your enemy.' But I say to you, Love your enemies and pray for those who persecute you, so that you may be children of your Father in heaven; for he makes his sun rise on the evil and on the good, and sends rain on the righteous and on the unrighteous . . . . Be perfect, therefore, as your heavenly Father is perfect" (Matt. 5:43–45, 48; cf. Luke 6:27–28, 35–36). Jesus bases his command for love against hate toward enemies on the character of God, thereby contradicting the character of God assumed in Psalms 5 and 11.

One might call the correction offered by Jesus "progressive revelation," on the ground that this revelation corrects a previous revelation. It is arguable, however, that the previous characterization of God, in Psalms 5 and 11, is not a revelation from God at all. It is arguably a human misunderstanding of God, a false characterization, stemming from a hateful human attitude toward enemies. We do not have evidence, in any case, that it comes from a God worthy of worship. On the contrary, the hateful attitude toward enemies ascribed to God contradicts a perfectly good moral character required for worthiness of worship and full trust.

We need to use corrective discernment to get a consistent and tenable portrait of a God worthy of worship from the Biblical writings. We need to separate the wheat from the chaff, because the chaff of an evil, hateful god is present in various Biblical contexts. The same holds for interpreting God's character across other religious traditions. We thus need candor about our need for corrective discernment, as shown by Jesus. Otherwise, we will fail to avoid a hateful or otherwise evil characterization of God that contradicts worthiness of worship. We cannot escape this demand for discernment if we are to think of God as morally perfect and worthy of worship. The problem results from morally degraded human influence in the Biblical writings and in other scriptural and religious traditions. Having set the bar high, we are looking for the character of a God worthy of worship, not a portrait of a god corroded by human hate or other human evil toward people.

An early statement of a divine goal for guidance occurs in the Genesis story of Abraham: "I will indeed bless you, and I will make your offspring as numerous as the stars of heaven and as the sand that is on the seashore. And your offspring shall possess the gate of their enemies, and by your offspring shall all the nations of the earth gain blessing for themselves" (Gen. 22:17–18). A previous announcement of such a universal divine goal is: "I will bless those who bless you, and the one who curses you I will curse; and in you all the families [מִשְׁפְּחֹת; *miš-pə-ḥōṯ*] of the earth shall be blessed" (Gen. 12:3).

Abraham's God thus has a broad scope of positive concern for all humans and their families, and this is atypical for divine perspectives in ancient times.

The core divine goal of the promise to Abraham is: "All the families of the earth shall be blessed." This is a sign of divine altruism, a concern for the well-being of all families, including all people, on earth. So, Abraham's God is no mere clan god or national god. His God seeks to benefit all nations and families of the earth, thus countering exclusive national and ethnic gods. Divine election of a particular people for a particular purpose, such as reaching other people, does not contradict this aim. Positive universal concern fits with worthiness of worship, as it excludes national, ethnic, and racial bias in vital matters for humans. Whatever the historical details about Abraham (and they are historically elusive), the book of Genesis presents a God of Abraham whose universal promise of human benefit agrees with altruism and worthiness of worship. (The evidence of divine altruism in the God of Abraham is neglected by Coogan [2019]. For discussion of divine blessings for nations outside Israel, see Fretheim [2005: chapter 4] and Brueggemann [2009: chapter 4].)

The promise from Abraham's God stems from a divine aim to build a universal family as a commonwealth reflective of God's moral character. *The Oxford English Dictionary, 3d ed.,* offers the following definition of "commonwealth": "the people of a nation, state, etc., as a whole; a state, nation, or independent community, especially viewed as an entity in which the whole population has a voice or interest." It also offers a relevant definition of "commonweal": "common well-being; especially the general good, welfare, or prosperity of a community or country as a whole." A God worthy of worship would seek commonweal as "common well-being" in righteousness, that is, "the general welfare" in righteousness of the community of people "as a whole." Otherwise, God would be guilty of a moral failure of undue bias against some people. Abraham's God seems not to harbor such a bias, at least given the promise of universal blessing across all families and nations.

Paul understands the God of Abraham to seek a universal commonwealth under divine righteousness in a "family of faith." He asks, and answers: "Is God the God of Jews only? Is he not the God of Gentiles also? Yes, of Gentiles also, since God is one; and he will justify the circumcised on the ground of faith and the uncircumcised through that same faith" (Rom. 3:29–30; cf. Rom. 1:16–17). Paul adds: "There is no distinction between Jew and Greek; the same Lord is Lord of all and is generous to all who call on him" (Rom. 10:12; cf. Rom. 4:16–17).

In Paul's message of good news, the God of Abraham provides a means to include all people, Gentiles as well as Jews, in the divine commonwealth as a family of faith. (See Dodd [1920]; cf. Dodd [1970: 90–91].) So, he does not take God's "election" of the Jews to exclude non-Jewish people from the intended family of God. On the contrary, he regards the divine election of the Jews to be a means to expand the family of God to Gentiles, without their conversion to Judaism. (This Pauline theme is neglected by Coogan [2019]; for a more accurate treatment, see Mikva [2020: chapters 8 and 9] and Dunn [1998: 509–32]. On some Greek and Roman approaches to divine guidance during Paul's time, see Jillions [2020: Part 1].)

Paul remarks: "So I ask, have they [the Jewish people] stumbled so as to fall? By no means! But through their stumbling salvation has come to the Gentiles, so as to make Israel jealous. Now if their stumbling means riches for the world, and if their defeat means riches for Gentiles, how much more will their full inclusion mean!" (Rom. 11:11–12). Paul identifies human unbelief, or distrust, toward God as the source of such stumbling (Rom. 11:20), but he portrays God as inviting reconciliation nonetheless: "Of Israel he [God] says, 'All day long I have held out my hands to a disobedient and contrary people'" (Rom. 10:21; cf. Isa. 65:2).

The building of the divine commonwealth as a family of faith depends, according to Paul, on divine mercy and on humans allowing it to lead to their repentance (Rom. 2:4). As a result, humans can opt out, thereby frustrating God's redemptive plan for them. The divine commonwealth depends, then, on voluntary human cooperation, and not just on divine power. Divine guidance, contrary to many interpreters, is not "sovereign" in a way that contradicts this consideration about human responsibility.

Paul's portrait of the merciful God of Abraham is not shared by all interpreters, but that is no surprise. We have noted the need to use discernment toward our available evidence regarding God. This is true not only for the Biblical evidence of God's character but also for the evidence of God's character in extra-Biblical religious traditions. For instance, the vicious interpretation of Allah's character by ISIS (Daesh) is not representative of God for Islam in general. Similarly, the caste-discriminating interpretation of God's (Brahma's) character by some Hindu traditions does not guide all variations of Hinduism. Likewise, a Calvinist doctrine of full divine causation does not fit with all Christian approaches to providence. Analogous lessons apply to theistic traditions at large. Treatment of relevant evidence among interpreters proceeds sometimes in mutually incompatible ways, for better or worse. Not all interpreting, however, is equally good at accommodating our historical evidence or our relevant experience. In addition, not all interpreting aims to give a fair hearing, as we do, to a morally robust conception of a God worthy of worship who offers divine guidance to humans.

Seeking for Faith

Abraham's God, according to Jesus, does not take membership in the divine commonwealth lightly. This God does not remain passive but actively seeks after people to include them in God's family:

> [Jesus] told them this parable: "Which one of you, having a hundred sheep and losing one of them, does not leave the ninety-nine in the wilderness and go after the one that is lost until he finds it? When he has found it, he lays it on his shoulders and rejoices. And when he comes home, he calls together his friends and neighbors, saying to them, 'Rejoice with me, for I have found my sheep that was lost.' Just so, I tell you, there will be more joy in heaven over one sinner who repents than over ninety-nine righteous persons who need no repentance." (Luke 15:3–7; cf. Matt. 18:10–14, Ezek. 34:11–16)

What, then, is it like to be God in relating to humans, according to Jesus? It is like being the shepherd who goes after his lost sheep to bring them home, rejoicing when they cooperate. Although rare among ancient images of God, this portrait motivates the message and mission of Jesus regarding God. Jesus applied a similar portrait of seeking others to himself as God's beloved son and representative (Luke 19:10; cf. Matt. 18:11). He did so to reflect, in a filial manner, God's character worthy of worship. This effort stemmed in part from his searching the Jewish scriptures for the God he experienced as "Abba."

Matthew's Gospel portrays Jesus as God's approved filial representative for a universal search for God's family members: "Jesus came and said to them, 'All authority in heaven and on earth has been given to me. Go therefore and make disciples of all nations, baptizing them in the name of the Father and of the Son and of the Holy Spirit, and teaching them to obey everything that I have commanded you'" (Matt. 28:18–20; cf. Luke 24:45–49). This universal scope for the divine commonwealth, drawing from "all nations," is required by God's being worthy of worship. It blocks undue bias against candidates for God's family. The dominant view among New Testament writers, in promoting outreach to Gentiles, is that the universal mission of Jesus opposes such bias..

If God settled for a narrow scope for the family commonwealth, a charge of moral inadequacy would arise, at least from the morally perfect standpoint of worthiness of worship. The moral status of God's righteousness then would be questionable, as suggested by the Hebrew prophetic tradition that understands such righteousness to be devoted to salvation across nations. For instance, the book of Isaiah represents God to announce: "Turn to me and be saved, all the ends of the earth! For I am God, and there is no other. By myself I have sworn, from my mouth has gone forth in righteousness a word that shall not return: 'To me every knee shall bow, every tongue shall swear'" (Isa. 45:22–23; cf. Rom. 14:10–12).

Despite the plea of Isaiah's God to humans, Jesus had doubts about its full success: "When the Son of Man comes, will he find faith on earth?" (Luke 18:8). His doubts stemmed from human failings in response to his message, and not God's intentions. So, divine guidance can fail in its purpose, given human lack of cooperation.

Human attitudes and motives matter for membership in God's family commonwealth, according to Jesus and Paul, and one expected motive is faith in God. The relevant notion of faith is controversial, however, with some interpreters emphasizing intellectual assent and others focusing on trust in God. Some of Paul's remarks suggest trust in God as a main component, after the example of Abraham: "What does the scripture say? 'Abraham believed God, and it was reckoned to him as righteousness . . . .' To one who without works trusts him who justifies the ungodly, such faith is reckoned as righteousness" (Rom. 4:3, 5). Trust in the God of the divine commonwealth, according to Paul, is thus the way to membership in that community.

Paul identifies faith, including trust, in God to be God's approved means to include people, even those outside Israel, in God's redeemed family: "For this reason it depends on faith, in order that the promise may rest on grace and be guaranteed to all his [Abraham's] descendants, not only to the adherents of the law but also to those who share the faith of Abraham (for he is the father of all of us, as it is written, 'I have made you the father of many nations')" (Rom. 4:16–17). In Paul's perspective, God aims to extend the family commonwealth beyond Israel as a gift, by means of human faith in God. This aim leaves any person of such faith, whether Jew or Gentile, as an approved member of God's family.

Paul holds that faith in God is the divinely approved way to receive God's guiding Spirit as a gift and thereby the distinctive fruit of the Spirit, including divine love (Gal. 3:2–5, 5:22–24). Faith as trust, according to Paul's message, thus enables divine righteous love to empower and guide humans to extend God's commonwealth in a way reflective of God's moral character. So, according to Paul, God supplies as a gift the empowering means and guidance to build the promised commonwealth, and such means and guidance rely on a cooperative human response of faith in God. God first self-presents to receptive humans (in God's preferred time), showing them divine goodness in some way, and they then respond, ideally, with faith's cooperation.

Paul thinks of a person who responds cooperatively with faith in God to be led, or guided, by God and thereby to be a receptive child of God: "All who are led by the Spirit of God are children of God" (Rom. 8:14). Being thus led includes one's putting to death, with God's power, one's own evil deeds opposed to God (Rom. 8:13). God thereby seeks humans willing to be adopted as children into God's family: "You have not received a spirit of slavery leading to fear again, but you have received a spirit of adoption as sons and daughters by which we cry out, 'Abba! Father!'" (Rom. 8:15, NASB; cf. Gal. 4:6).

In Paul's message of good news, God seeks a filial relationship with potential members of the universal commonwealth, whereby they are willingly led by God as their righteous Father. The desired filial model is exemplified by Jesus in Gethsemane, who prays to God: "Abba, Father, for you all things are possible; remove this cup from me; yet, not what I want, but what you want" (Mark 14:36). (See Moser [2021b: chapter 3].) Faith in God would lose its reception of divine motivating power without this filial attitude of obeying God. So, faith in God includes trusting God with willingness to cooperate with God for the sake of righteousness in action.

Humans may or may not willingly receive the uncoercive divine power offered for divine guidance. Sometimes, Paul observes, we "quench the Spirit" of God (1 Thess. 5:19; cf. Eph. 4:30), and we thus "frustrate the grace of God" (Gal. 2:21). In that case, divine guidance fails to lead us, as a result of our failure. In contrast, when we cooperate, in Paul's perspective, the divine moral power in our experience becomes our motivation for action, as well as our foundational evidence of God's reality and guidance. Our cooperation then enables the divine power on offer to come to fruition in our lives, thus becoming what it is intended by God to be: a source of an actively righteous relationship with God and others. Inquirers disagree about whether there actually is such power in our experience, and this is understandable. The presence of this power, as suggested, can vary as a result of variation in human readiness to receive it. It also can vary as a result of God's timing for its best opportunity for being offered. God thus can hide divine self-manifestation accordingly, until a person is ready to receive it cooperatively. Divine guidance can vary accordingly.

Guided Divine Conflict

The God of Abraham, according to Jesus and Paul, seeks cooperation from wayward humans despite their ongoing conflict against divine righteousness. This tendency is at the heart of the Biblical portrait of divine mercy and grace needed by humans. The divine goal for a universal commonwealth faces stubborn opposition from powers, individual and social, at odds with God's active moral character and will. As a result, the God of Abraham, as portrayed by Jesus and Paul, creates conflict and even some human suffering for the sake of attracting and leading people to divine righteousness in their relationships. For instance, Paul remarks: "The creation was subjected to futility, not of its own will but by the will of the one who subjected it, in hope that the creation itself will be set free from its bondage to decay and will obtain the freedom of the glory of the children of God" (Rom 8:20–21). This "subjecting to futility" is part of the divine effort to lead humans to righteousness in their relationships to God and other humans.

Paul has in mind at least the will of moral agents in creation subjected to futility and their corresponding suffering, given his mention of a "will" in "its own will." His point is that God sometimes frustrates at least anti-God wills among humans in order to provide a way for the benefit, including the liberation, of people willing to be cooperative children of God. God thus creates and uses redemptive conflict and suffering for the good of the desired filial commonwealth. Paul's God, then, is no largely passive god of Plato, Aristotle, or the deists.

God, according to Paul, is active in redemptive conflict for the sake of righteousness among and within "the children of God." Paul thinks of this righteousness to include people being "conformed [by God] to the image of his Son, in order that he might be the firstborn within a large family" (Rom. 8:29; cf. 1 Cor. 1:30). Paul regards being voluntarily attracted to conformity to the righteous image of Jesus, after the model of Gethsemane, to be the ideal for divine leading to righteousness in humans and their relationships.

The righteous God of the Jewish scriptures engages in conflict not only with wayward humans but also with competing gods. Psalm 82 represents such cosmic conflict involving God:

> God has taken his place in the divine council;
> in the midst of the gods he holds judgment:
> "How long will you judge unjustly
> and show partiality to the wicked?
> Give justice to the weak and the orphan;
> maintain the right of the lowly and the destitute.
> Rescue the weak and the needy;
> deliver them from the hand of the wicked."
> They have neither knowledge nor understanding,
> they walk around in darkness;
> all the foundations of the earth are shaken . . . .
> Rise up, O God, judge the earth;
> for all the nations belong to you! (Psalm 82:1–5, 8)

This God judges the lesser gods for their moral inadequacy, for their deficit in righteousness, including social justice. As a result, this God challenges the unrighteous ways of those gods. Divine conflict serves that purpose, including in human lives, for the sake of God's righteous commonwealth.

We should expect evidence for a righteous God's reality and guidance to include an experience of intentional conflict from God against unrighteousness in our lives. The final conquest of such unrighteousness would come at God's timing, but it would begin with conflict in advance of full conquest, given human participation and its limitations. We humans, in any case, would not be in a position to set God's specific means or timing or for a final resolution. We would have, however, the option to cooperate with the righteous conflict for the benefit of the divine commonwealth, and that option could inform the meaning and the divine guidance of human life.

The Jewish Bible portrays God as a "devouring fire" against human unrighteousness and as "jealous" (in a way explained below) over maintaining and guiding toward divine righteousness (Deut. 4:24–25; cf. Ex. 20:5, 24:17). Paul likewise expresses the divine seriousness about matters of righteousness: "The Lord is an avenger in all these things, just as we have already told you beforehand and solemnly warned you. For God did not call us to impurity but in holiness. Therefore whoever rejects this rejects not human authority but God" (1 Thess. 4:6–8). In Paul's perspective, then, human reception of God must accommodate and conform to divine righteousness. The same holds for being guided by God.

Before Paul, Jesus reflected the image of God as devourer in the Jewish Bible, portraying himself to bring the transforming fire of divine righteousness: "From everyone to whom much has been given, much will be required; and from the one to whom much has been entrusted, even more will be demanded. I came to bring fire to the earth" (Luke 12:48–49). Following Isaiah 29:13, Jesus portrays God's intended righteousness and jealousy to extend to the inward life, the "hearts," of humans: "This people honors me with their lips, but their hearts are far from me . . . . It is what comes out of a person that defiles. For it is from within, from the human heart, that evil intentions come: fornication, theft, murder, adultery, avarice, wickedness, deceit, licentiousness, envy, slander, pride, folly. All these evil things come from within, and they defile a person" (Mark 7:6, 20–23). They defile, according to Jesus, because they alienate people from God and God's righteous will, and thus from the divine kingdom (Matt. 7:17–21).

The concern of Jesus, on behalf of God, for the inward life of humans echoes a plea from a Jewish Psalm: "Search me, O God, and know my heart; test me and know my thoughts. See if there is any wicked way in me, and lead me in the way everlasting" (Psalm 139:23–24). The *way* "everlasting" that includes inwardness recalls a theme from Psalm 23:3: "He restores my soul. He leads me in paths of righteousness for his name's sake." The prophets Jeremiah and Ezekiel saw the human need for such inward divine restoration and leading (Jer. 24:7, 31:33–34; Ezek. 36:24–28). The divine restoration and leading, in their perspective, include a battle in a human soul for the human "heart," including conscience.

The divine battle's center concerns divine righteousness on offer in human moral experience. The divine aim is to renew and guide people, individually and socially, via their cooperation with the attractive power of the gift of divine righteousness presented in their experience. The needed power to renew and guide in that way does not come from humans themselves; its source, according to Jesus and Paul, is divine.

Conscience as Battleground

Paul regards human conscience as fallible but as a place to receive testimony from God and to have it confirmed by God. Conscience is not uniformly the voice of God and thus needs to be approached with discernment for righteousness. Even so, Paul relies on it for receiving divine guidance: "I am speaking the truth in Christ – I am not lying; my conscience confirms it by the Holy Spirit" (Rom. 9:1). God's Spirit, in this perspective, confirms things in human conscience, even though it is a place of conflict and struggle over divine righteousness. Conscience, according to Paul, bears witness in many cases to divine righteousness, including the righteousness expressed by the law of God (Rom. 2:15). He thinks of the reality of conscience to involve his "inmost self" as a place of conflict: "I delight in the law of God in my inmost self, but I see in my members another law at war with the law of my mind, making me captive to the law of sin that dwells in my members" (Rom. 7:22–23). The problem of human moral failure, then, is not to be blamed on the law of God, according to Paul. The same holds for the human problem of failing to be guided by God. (On Paul on the inward conflict and on legalism, see Timmins [2017] and Sanders [1983: 154–62].)

Paul regards the "war" within to include a conflict in conscience between the moral power of the Spirit of God and the power of sin as being "according to flesh" (κατὰ σάρκα). Human conscience, in his perspective, reflects this ongoing conflict between moral attitudes for and against divine righteousness:

> Those who live according to the flesh [κατὰ σάρκα] set their minds on the things of the flesh, but those who live according to the Spirit set their minds on the things of the Spirit. To set the mind on the flesh is death, but to set the mind on the Spirit is life and peace. For this reason the mind that is set on the flesh is hostile to God; it does not submit to God's law – indeed it cannot, and those who are in the flesh cannot please God. (Rom. 8:5–8)

The Spirit of God in this conflict offers life in divine righteousness, as opposed to death in alienation from God (Rom. 8:10). Paul himself experiences this ongoing conflict in conscience, where there is often a struggle between righteous and unrighteous attitudes and options for action. Divine guidance aims to lead people through such struggle, toward righteousness in relationships.

We now have a psychological context for discerning the reality and the guidance of the Biblical God of righteousness: our moral experience, including our conscience, that presents a conflict and a choice for us between righteousness and unrighteousness. This experience can include the intended divine leading toward righteousness identified previously. For instance, it can present repeated nudging and attracting of our will in that direction, without coercion. We still remain morally responsible agents in the conflict, and we can decide and struggle for one side or the other. We thus can choose either to cooperate or not to cooperate with divine guidance.

Imagine a situation where some people choose to cooperate with divine righteousness found in their moral experience. They should expect to gain in due course less mixed, more salient evidence of God's moral character, of what God is like morally, on the assumption that God aims to support their cooperation. In that case, they would allow divine moral power to come to fruition in their experience, thereby apprehending its distinctive function in favor of righteousness in relationships. Their choice between God and what is anti-God then would be set in sharper relief, even if they fail to categorize it as involving God.

God could be present *de re*, as an influential reality, in human moral experience without a *de dicto* component of human classification of the relevant power *as God*. Divine moral power would not depend for its reality or influence on human understanding or categorization. So, diversity in religious belief could arise despite similar underlying religious experiences of divine moral power. God, then, could work across differing, even conflicting, religious belief-systems by presenting common evidence of God and divine moral power in human experience. (See Moser [2021c].)

We would miss what it would be like to be God morally if we neglected the divine role of seeking and presenting conflict for righteousness in human moral experience, including conscience. We then could miss out on recognizing actual experiential evidence for God and even decide not to take the prospect of God's reality seriously. As a result, we may become inclined to represent the world, including our lives, as devoid of God and thus of a source of lasting meaning for human life. In that case, our moral struggle could be tempered by our cynicism about life's long-term value, especially when the struggle is intense and demanding. Going against the model set by Jesus, we then may opt for our own will rather than God's in our Gethsemane struggles over righteousness. We have the dangerous freedom to suppress our conscience in the grips of such struggles, thereby shutting out divine activity intended to be redemptive for us. When exercised thus, our freedom can result in our failing to discern God's reality and guidance. The matter is complicated by danger from God.

Peril in Guidance

Discerning the reality of a worthy God is a variation of seeking for such a God. Jesus commanded such seeking: "Seek first [God's] kingdom and his righteousness" (Matt. 6:33, RSV). He added a promise for the search: "Seek, and you will find . . . . For he who seeks finds" (Matt. 7:7–8, RSV; cf. Jer. 29:13). Why did he command such seeking? Part of the answer is that it enables a person to become "fit for the kingdom of God" (Luke 9:62). It can bring needed focus of attention and value-priority for a person, of the kind required by this command from Jesus: "Enter by the narrow gate; for the gate is wide, and the way is easy, that leads to destruction, and those who enter by it are many. For the gate is narrow and the way is hard, that leads to life" (Matt. 7:13–14). The hardness, according to Jesus, stems from God's morally demanding moral character and human resistance to it.

Given a narrow gate of divine righteousness, we should expect God to try to purify people toward focusing on, and cooperating with, such righteousness (cf. Amos 9:9). If God first loved humans before they loved God, they should expect God to try to find them, in getting their attention, before they look for God. God thus would challenge available humans for the sake of their becoming righteous, intending for them to seek God with due priority. Seeking the inward righteous life of a person, Jesus remarked that "where your treasure is, there will your heart be also" (Matt. 6:21; cf. Luke 12:34). Seeking for God with due openness to and valuing of divine righteousness can help to direct a person's "heart" toward such righteousness. It thus can prepare a person to become fit for divine righteousness and God's kingdom family.

Seeking for God could point inquirers successfully in a Godward direction, but it need not. They could come up empty with needed evidence of God's reality and guidance. The timing for the presentation of such evidence to humans would be at God's discretion, without a recipe for humans. In addition, seeking does not serve as an end in itself. Ideally, when needed evidence emerges, it gives way to human cooperation with the God aiming for a righteous commonwealth. The power of such a God then can come to fruition in human experience as salient and redemptive for its recipients. That God would act for the sake of righteousness among humans, and recipients would be expected to follow suit, in a way that goes beyond thinking and interpreting, toward benefiting a commonwealth of agents.

As expected, we have no full understanding of God's ways and hence no theodicy of full explanation. That lack, however, would not undermine the experiential evidence some inquirers find in moral experience. The best available explanation of their moral experience would acknowledge divine leading there, even though the experience of others could call for a different explanation. Experience, evidence, and explanation can vary in that way, even given the guiding activity of a good God. (See Moser [2020: chapters 7 and 8]). Section 3 returns to this topic.)

If we seek aright for a worthy God and find success, we can break the cycle of mere speculation about divine reality and bring attention, including awareness, to divine power in our moral experience. That power would show us what it is like to be a God worthy of worship and trust, and it would guide us to a fitting response. We then would appreciate the value of Paul's concern that "your faith might rest not on human wisdom but on the power of God" (1 Cor. 2:5). We also would begin to appreciate the value of Jesus's aforementioned command and promise: Seek, and you will find. Even so, an obstacle is the peril in the process, resulting from divine zeal and jealousy. We need to factor in such peril to understand divine guidance.

The divine zeal shown by the Biblical God fits with the following definition and examples (with dates) from the *Oxford English Dictionary, 3d ed.:*

> Passion, fervour; vehemence of feeling … . In Biblical language, as an attribute of God: passionate love or care which will tolerate no unfaithfulness or disobedience. Cf. jealousy, jealous adj. 1382: *Bible* (Wycliffite, E.V.) (Douce 370) (1850) 4 Kings xix. 31: The zeel [1425 L.V. feruent loue, 1535 Coverdale gelousy; L. zelus] of the Lord of hoostis schal done that …. 1611: *Bible (*King James*)*Ezek. v. 13: They shal know that I the Lord haue spoken it in my zeale, when I haue accomplished my fury in them.

The zeal fitting for God is captured also by a definition of "violence" in the OED: "Vehemence or intensity of emotion, behaviour, or language; extreme fervour; passion." We should prefer talk of divine zeal to talk of divine violence, however, because talk of violence suggests to many users of English something evil rather than good. The term "zeal" does not have the latter negative connotation. It can connote, for instance, intensity for righteousness, including in interpersonal relationships.

John's Gospel portrays Jesus's disciples as recognizing zeal for God in his cleansing of the temple:

> The Passover of the Jews was near, and Jesus went up to Jerusalem. In the temple he found people selling cattle, sheep, and doves, and the money changers seated at their tables. Making a whip of cords, he drove all of them out of the temple, both the sheep and the cattle. He also poured out the coins of the money changers and overturned their tables. He told those who were selling the doves, "Take these things out of here! Stop making my

Father's house a marketplace!" His disciples remembered that it was written,
"Zeal [ζῆλος] for your house will consume me." (John 2:13–17)

The reference to what "was written" is to Psalm 69:9: "It is zeal for your house
that has consumed me; the insults of those who insult you have fallen on me."
Jesus, according to his disciples in John's Gospel, was consumed by such zeal
for God and God's house.

The Gospels of Mark and Matthew understand Jesus to be protecting God's
temple as a house of prayer:

> On reaching Jerusalem, Jesus entered the temple courts and began driving out
> those who were buying and selling there. He overturned the tables of the
> money changers and the benches of those selling doves, and would not allow
> anyone to carry merchandise through the temple courts. And as he taught
> them, he said, "Is it not written: 'My house will be called a house of prayer for
> all nations'? But you have made it 'a den of robbers'".
>
> (Mark 11:15–18; cf. Matt. 21:12–13)

The background here for the Gospels of Mark and Matthew is Isaiah 56:7:
"These I will bring to my holy mountain, and make them joyful in my house of
prayer; their burnt offerings and their sacrifices will be accepted on my altar; for
my house shall be called a house of prayer for all peoples." The background also
includes Jeremiah 7:11: "Has this house, which is called by my name, become
a den of robbers in your sight? You know, I too am watching, says the Lord."
Jesus thus undertakes zealous (and, in *that* sense, "violent") righteous action for
God and God's temple, in order to protect the temple as a house of prayer. He
understands God to approve such zealous action.

Jesus portrays God not merely to approve but also to undertake zealous
action for the sake of divine righteousness among humans. The high point of
such action is God's sending Jesus, as confirmed at the Last Supper and in
Gethsemane, to go to Jerusalem to die for God's self-sacrificial mission to
redeem people. Such divine action, in the giving of God's beloved Son, shows
unsurpassed zeal for righteousness in the divine redemption of wayward
people.

Divine zeal for righteousness emerges in God's warning people of impending
judgment for their unrighteousness. Jesus illustrates that factor in some of his
parables of judgment (Matt. 13:24–30, 36–43, 47–50, 25:31–46). The God of
Jesus, then, is zealous in acting for righteousness among humans, because that
God is righteous, and vehemently so. This God contrasts sharply here with the
aloof god of deism. (On divine righteousness, see Snaith [1944: chapters 2 and 3];
Knight [1959: chapters 8, 20]; Williams [1980]; Hultgren [1985: 12–46]; Bird
[2006: chapters 2, 4].)

The book of Isaiah, formative for Jesus and for many New Testament writers, gives a straightforward endorsement of divine holiness in terms of righteousness: "The Lord of hosts is exalted by justice, and the Holy God shows himself holy by righteousness" (Isa. 5:16). The book of Isaiah also assumes the moral excellence of God's holiness in contrasting such holiness with Isaiah's "unclean lips" (Isa. 6:1–5). According to this book, divine righteousness bears directly on interpersonal moral relationships, including divine–human moral relationships. Divine zeal in action is for the sake of such good moral relationships, in keeping with God's distinctive moral character. This consideration fits with God's response to Moses's request to see divine glory (כְּבֹדֶךָ): God replies with a show of divine goodness (טוּבִי) (Ex. 33:18–19).

God's zeal for righteousness among humans stems from divine jealousy *over* them, for their sake, but not jealousy *of* them. The OED offers a definition of "jealous" that bears on divine jealousy over humans for the sake of righteousness: "Vehement in feeling, as in wrath, desire, or devotion." In addition:

> Zealous or solicitous for the preservation or well-being of something possessed or esteemed; vigilant or careful in guarding; suspiciously careful or watchful. Const. *of* (*for, over*). 1526: *Bible* (Tyndale) 2 Cor. xi. 2: I am gelous over you with godly gelousy. . . . In biblical language, said of God: Having a love which will tolerate no unfaithfulness or defection in the beloved object. 1382: *Bible* (Wycliffite, E.V.) Exod. xx. 5: I forsothe am the Lord thi God, strong gelows [1425 *L.V.* a stronge gelouse louyere]. 1535: *Bible* (Coverdale) Exod. xx. 5: For I the Lorde thy God am a gelouse God. 1535: *Bible* (Coverdale) Josh. Xxiv: He is an holy God, mightie, and gelous, which spareth not youre trangressions and synnes.

Such divine jealousy motivates divine zeal in guidance toward humans, with the goal of righteousness in divine–human relations.

God's jealousy is over people for the sake of their righteousness in relating to God and others. That, however, is not its ultimate basis. The foundation is in God's jealousy over God's own character of righteousness. Ezekiel thus represents God to say: "I will be jealous for my holy name" (Ezek. 39:25). The "holy name" includes God's unique righteous character, the basis for divine zeal and jealousy extended to human relationships with God. God thus protects, jealously, God's unique character of righteousness. [The Hebrew word in the Jewish scriptures often translated as "jealous" (*qannā*, קַנָּא) is often translated also as "zealous," with context being the key determinant.]

Walther Eichrodt has noted the widespread idea of divine jealousy in the Jewish scriptures:

> The characteristic note of all those statements concerning the divine operation determined by the Sinai revelation is the fearful dynamic of the divine

demands. The description of God as "*êl qannā*" [jealous (אֵל קַנָּא)] (Ex. 20.5, 34.14) exactly hits off this impression. But even where this precise term is not found, it is nevertheless the idea of the jealous God which determines the whole slant of Mosaic religion, with its passionate striving for Yahweh's sole dominion and the total subjugation of man to his will.

(1961: vol. 1, 209–10)

Eichrodt adds that "it is impossible to limit this feature simply to one single period of Israelite religion. It must be recognized as the basic element in the whole OT idea of God" (1961: vol. 1, 210). Divine jealousy thus looms large in the portrait of YHWH in the Jewish scriptures. This is not a god of moral indifference or complacency. Instead, we are faced with a living, convicting God of moral fervor and corresponding zeal in action. (In support, Eichrodt mentions: Josh. 24:19, Deut. 4:24, 5:9f., 6:15, 32:16, 21, Num. 25:1, Nahum 1:2, Zeph. 1:18, 3:8, Ezek. 5:13, 16:42, 23:25, 36:5f., 38:19, 39:25, Isa. 59:17, 63:15, Zech. 1:14, 8:2, Joel 2:18. On the exclusive demand of the first commandment of the decalogue, see Miller [2009: chapter 1].)

The Epistle of James asks: "Do you suppose that it is for nothing that the scripture says, "God yearns jealously for the spirit that he has made to dwell in us?" (James 4:5). The writer of this epistle is protesting against spiritual "adultery" for the sake of righteous loyalty to God. Such adultery invites divine jealousy and anger, as some of the Psalms indicate. For instance: "They provoked [God] to anger with their high places; they moved him to jealousy with their idols" (Psalm 78:5). Another Psalm asks: "How long, O Lord? Will you be angry forever? Will your jealous wrath burn like fire?" (Psalm 79:5). In a similar vein, Paul asks: "Are we provoking the Lord to jealousy? Are we stronger than he?" (1 Cor 10:22). Such passages assume that God is ultimately jealous over God's unique moral character and, on that basis, jealous over God's people, to the point of anger where appropriate.

According to the New Testament gospels, Jesus shares in divine jealousy for righteousness, including in human commitment to him. He comments: "Whoever loves father or mother more than me is not worthy of me; and whoever loves son or daughter more than me is not worthy of me" (Matt. 10:37; cf. Luke 14:26). In addition: "None of you can become my disciple if you do not give up all your possessions" (Luke 14:33). In representing God as his Father, Jesus understands discipleship, and thus being guided by God, to require undivided loyalty to himself and God. This requirement emerges not only in his first love command (cited in the next section) but also in some of his parables that indicate God's attitude toward loyalty and jealousy for righteousness in relationships. The latter parables include the parables of the lost sheep, the marriage feast, and the talents (Matt. 18:10–14, 22:1–14, 25:14–30).

Terence Fretheim has characterized the relation between divine jealousy and undivided loyalty in connection with Exodus 34:14 (quoted on p. 15 above):

> God names himself with the metaphor Jealous, indicating that Israel's faithfulness is a matter close to the divine heart. This is not simply a formal matter with God. It touches God's very emotional life. It has to do not only with what God expects *from* Israel but, with an inescapable reference to the divine inwardness, what God feels for the people – jealousy by definition has both an inner and an outer reference. But *the inner reference is the prior one.* God cares deeply about Israel, and *because of that,* cares about what Israel does with its allegiances . . . . Because of the nature of jealousy, God's being moved [by human disobedience] will entail both pain and anger (1991: 309–10).

These remarks suggest that divine jealousy stems from God's caring, and God cares for the moral lives of people as well as God's own moral character and life. So, divine jealousy extends over people, particularly God's people, and God's unique moral character.

Jon D. Levenson has characterized divine jealousy as a response to attempted theft from God:

> God's jealousy is a response to baseless and fraudulent claims by others upon things that belong to him alone. It is analogous to the response of the victim of identity theft or adultery. Were the victim to keep silent or to grant instantaneous forgiveness, the fraud and deceit would only grow, with devastating consequences for all involved . . . . To allow [other gods] the position rightly held by God alone is to debase the currency of his relationship with Israel . . . . Some things can, and should, be shared. Others simply cannot (2016: 10–11).

God's status of rightful authority is protected by divine jealousy, as is divine righteousness. Indeed, that authority is grounded in divine righteousness, owing to God's status of being worthy of worship, in being "God." Compromise of that status would be compromise in being God. It would leave theology fractured and debased at its core, and it would leave human morality without a basis in perfect righteousness.

Divine jealousy over humans contrasts with the envious or grudging attitude indicated by this definition of "jealous" in the OED: "In respect of success or advantage: Apprehensive of losing some desired benefit through the rivalry of another; feeling ill-will towards another on account of some advantage or superiority which he possesses or may possess; grudging, envious. Const. *of* (the person, or the advantage)." Divine jealousy over humans does not include that kind of "ill will" toward humans. On the contrary, it seeks what is good for humans, by aiming for their being in a righteous relationship with God, by the standard of God's perfectly good character. It is thus free of God's being envious or grudging toward humans and of any such selfishness. We should understand divine guidance accordingly.

God's zeal and jealousy for the sake of divine righteousness entail that God is perilous, or dangerous, for humans who identify with unrighteousness. God, according to Paul, is out to have humans kill their own human deeds of unrighteousness (Rom. 8:13) and therefore is a peril for them. The OED presents the following definition and examples for "peril": "The position or condition of being imminently exposed to the chance of injury, loss, or destruction; risk, jeopardy, danger. Example: 1749: T. Smollett *Regicide* ii. viii. 28: Glory Is the fair Child of Peril. 1382: *Bible (*Wycliffite, E.V.*)* (Bodl. 959) 1 Paralip. [Chronicles] xi. 19: In perele of þer lijues þei broȝten to me watir, & for þis cause he wolde not drynke." We thus can talk of good, rather than bad, peril or danger, owing to a good divine motive and goal for it: for righteousness in divine–human relations. Divine guidance comes with good peril for humans.

Zeal and jealousy may or may not be good. Paul illustrates how zeal for God can go astray, when he says of himself: "as to zeal, a persecutor of the church" (Phil. 3:6). Paul says of his fellow Jews who reject Jesus: "They have a zeal for God, but it is not enlightened. For, being ignorant of the righteousness that comes from God, and seeking to establish their own, they have not submitted to God's righteousness" (Rom. 10:2–3). The standard for good zeal and jealousy is thus God's righteousness, and God demands human submission to that standard. We need to explore what underlies divine jealousy, particularly in relation to divine guidance of humans.

Filial Possession and Futility

Divine jealousy safeguards God's righteous divinity, both in relation to God's actions and in relation to the conduct of human moral agents. The Biblical God lays claim to humans in holding them responsible, jealously, to divine righteousness. This kind of responsibility arises not from human preference, but from God's being the God of all humans, Gentiles as well as Jews.

Paul asks and answers: "Is God the God of Jews only? Is he not the God of Gentiles also? Yes, of Gentiles also, since God is one" (Rom. 3:29–30). Similarly, Paul affirms: "There is no distinction between Jew and Greek; the same Lord is Lord of all and is generous to all who call on him" (Rom. 10:12). Paul cites Deuteronomy 32:21 to illustrate God's use of jealousy: "Again I ask, did Israel not understand? First Moses says, 'I will make you jealous of those who are not a nation; with a foolish nation I will make you angry'" (Rom. 10:19).

The passage in Deuteronomy from which Paul quotes is: "They made me jealous with what is no god, provoked me with their idols. So, I will make them jealous with what is no people, provoke them with a foolish nation." God became jealous over righteousness as a result of Israel's disloyalty toward God, and this prompted God to challenge Israel to share in that divine jealousy. Paul thinks of this as God's effort to invite Israel to turn back to filial cooperation with God (Rom. 10:21). Israel's jealousy toward the Gentiles is to stem from its jealousy over the Gentiles' newfound God, who is "generous to all who call on him."

God's commitment anchoring divine jealousy over humans is "I will be *your* God." It emerges for Israel as follows: "I will take you as my people, and I will be your God. You shall know that I am the Lord your God, who has freed you from the burdens of the Egyptians" (Ex. 6:7). Two factors are noteworthy. First, God's being "your God" entails God's "taking you as my people." Second, God anchors this "taking" in a prior divine intervention on behalf of the people in question. In the case of the Israelites under Moses, it was God's showing care and jealousy for them by leading them from the oppression of the Egyptians. So, divine guidance figured in the special evidence and knowledge Israel had of God as righteous, loving, and jealous. God, according to Paul, seeks to guide Gentiles in a similar manner.

Jesus associates himself with the liberating God of Israel, with his citing the following from the book of Isaiah:

> The Spirit of the Lord is upon me,
> because he has anointed me
> to bring good news to the poor.
> He has sent me to proclaim release to the captives
> and recovery of sight to the blind,
> to let the oppressed go free,
> to proclaim the year of the Lord's favor.
> (Luke 4:18–19; cf. Lev. 25:10, Isa. 61:1–2)

It thus should be no surprise that Jesus, as noted, upholds the kind of undivided loyalty to divine righteousness that is characteristic of God. He shares God's jealousy over such righteousness, including in relation to God's people. His emphasis on faith in God calls for cooperation with God's jealousy over righteousness.

In promoting full loyalty to God as father, Jesus assumes God's filial possession of his disciples, at least regarding their responsibilities and priorities. In short, they are owned by God, and they thus belong to God in terms of their responsibilities and priorities. Jesus suggests this in his first love command: "Hear, O Israel: the

Lord our God, the Lord is one; you shall love the Lord your God with all your heart, and with all your soul, and with all your mind, and with all your strength" (Mark 12:29–30). God's children, according to Jesus, owe God such full love, above all else, and they are to respond to divine guidance accordingly.

Jesus puts his disciples' primary responsibility to God bluntly in Luke's Gospel: "When you have done all that you were ordered to do, say, 'We are worthless slaves; we have done only what we ought to have done!'" (Luke 17:10). God's filial possession of the people of God, according to Jesus, is caring, but it also is demanding, jealously, of divine righteousness. In Matthew's Gospel, Jesus thus remarks: "Unless your righteousness exceeds that of the scribes and Pharisees, you will never enter the kingdom of heaven" (Matt. 5:20). In addition, as noted, Jesus commands: "Strive first for the kingdom of God and his righteousness" (Matt. 6:33). God, then, aims to build a kingdom family among humans, and that family is divinely protected, jealously, for righteousness. Divine ownership motivates this redemptive effort, including its divine guidance of humans.

An understanding of divine guidance should attend to its ultimate aim of God's filial possession of humans in their righteous cooperation with God. Otherwise, we risk portraying divine guidance as having a lesser end, such as informing humans or prompting human actions of obedience. We also should attend to the uncoercive character of divine guidance, acknowledging the human power to ignore or to resist such guidance. This factor enables humans to be responsible agents toward divine guidance. It also frees God from blame when humans oppose or neglect divine guidance. Even so, God allows for evil and mystery in the context of such guidance, and this results in cognitive dissonance in our explanatory efforts toward God and guidance. We turn now to such dissonance.

3 Guiding through Dissonance

> Do you not realize that God's goodness is meant to lead you to repentance?
> —Romans 2:4

Divine jealousy for guiding humans toward righteousness, we have suggested, leads to God's creating surprise, turbulence, and even woe for the sake of human moral improvement. This section will deny that we have a full explanatory theodicy for God's permitting suffering, but it will outline a different kind of theodicy we can have while preserving divine mystery of a sort. It also will suggest how divine guidance can proceed in the presence of dissonance from both good and evil.

Dissonance from Goodness

Given divine worthiness of worship, God's self-presentation of perfect moral goodness would be unique and thus would differ from the moral goodness typical of humans. It would indicate *God's* reality and guidance, thus differing from lesser manifestations of goodness in human experience, such as the goodness arising from a human. Divine self-manifestation of perfect goodness would not come to humans for their entertainment or amusement. Instead, it would bring God's perfect redemptive aim to wayward humans: the aim to attract them (more deeply) to divine–human reconciliation as agreeable cooperation with God. So, the self-manifestation would arise from an unfulfilled divine goal for humans, even if they are initially unclear about the goal and even if they oppose or neglect the goal.

The felt conflict between God's self-manifested moral character or will and a typical human moral character or will would include internal dissonance or discord in human experience. The OED offers the following definition of "dissonance": "want of concord or harmony (between things); disagreement, incongruity." It also offers this as a definition: "an inharmonious sound." Using auditory language, we might think of God's perfect character as yielding "an inharmonious sound" in the experience of a wayward human, stemming from its conflict with "the sound" of a morally inferior human character.

A key part of God's perfect moral character would be the perfect divine *will* regarding humans, that is, God's intentional resolve and plan toward humans. The divine will, in its moral perfection, would be incongruous with a wayward human will, and thus God's intervening good will would yield moral dissonance in human experience. We would have a conflict between two wills, one perfect and the other imperfect. From a moral point of view, God's will would have priority, with no serious moral challenge from an inferior human will.

Suppose that I intend to steal several butternut squash from the garden of my neighbor. He has boasted of his bumper crop of squash to me, and I have been tempted, with some jealousy, to visit his garden by night. My plan is to steal the squash in a way that indicates entrance from the yard of another neighbor. In the middle of the night, however, I am struck with a guilty conscience regarding my plan.

My conscience supplies, without coercion, volitional pressure against my intention to steal the squash. It gives me a sense of a morally better attitude toward my neighbor, and that sense attracts me and creates dissonance with my initial intention to steal the squash. My conscience presents a moral character and a will to me that conflict with my own character and will regarding my neighbor. It leaves me, then, with morally relevant dissonance in my moral experience. This experiential dissonance is part of my awareness, in attracting my attention, regardless of the decision I ultimately make about it.

My conscience leaves me with a decision to make regarding my conflicted experience in conscience. My options are:

(a) ignore the dissonance and divert my attention away from it,
(b) resist or oppose the volitional pressure to refrain from stealing squash from my neighbor,
(c) cooperate with the challenge to refrain from the stealing.

Options (a) and (b) would result in my failing to cooperate with the goodness manifested in my conscience. They are not the same decision, but from the standpoint of the presented goodness in my experience, they entail my being uncooperative. They amount to my deciding against God and the divine goodness presented in my moral experience.

The dissonance in my moral experience would not be just cognitive, a matter of conflicting pieces of knowledge, or even just doxastic, a matter of conflicting beliefs. It would go deeper, to my experiences that underlie my beliefs or knowledge. So, talk of either doxastic dissonance or cognitive dissonance would not capture the reality of my situation. An adequate phenomenology of my experience must attend to the features of my experience, regardless of what I know or believe about my experience. If God's will shows up in my experience, I should carefully assess my experience of it, even if my relevant knowledge or belief lags behind.

In my guilty conscience, I face corrective volitional pressure presented as part of my moral experience. Even if this pressure disturbs my sleep and my waking moments, it does not force my decision in response. It challenges me, in the experienced dissonance of goodness, not to steal from my neighbor, but I am left to respond freely. On careful reflection, relative to all of my available evidence, I consider the volitional pressure in conscience to be part of God's corrective will toward me. I have no indication that the pressure comes from my peers, teachers, family members, or other humans.

I have been presented with moral goodness that, by my evidence, manifests God's distinctive moral character, and this goodness goes against my initial will to steal from my neighbor. God's self-manifested will challenges me to care for my neighbor rather than to steal from him. It thus aims to frustrate my morally inferior will and character, for the sake of realizing God's better will toward righteousness. Morally, it convicts me of planned wrongdoing, seeking to attract me to cooperate with God's good will instead of my inferior will.

The presentation of a good will in my moral experience in conscience has a direction. It nudges me toward cooperative conviction, and it is best described, given my overall evidence, as *seeking to lead* me to cooperate with divine goodness. Its uncoercive nudging presents itself to me as goal-directed and thus as intentional. So, it does not simply present experiential content to be described by me. It presents a morally relevant volition that conflicts with my intention to steal, and it aims to attract me to forgo a decision to steal. Its intentional feature of goal-directedness indicates a person, an intentional agent, at work in the dissonance of my moral experience, and that agent is morally superior to me.

Only a person (or a personal agent) could *aim to lead* me. A mere object, event, idea, or feeling would not be intentional in that way. The person in question, however, differs from me, having a better will than mine, and that person's corrective will conflicts with my will. I can contradict my own will, but I am not doing so here; I am behind *only* the inferior will, at least initially. The better will is not my own will; it only meets my will with dissonance, seeking to frustrate my will to steal, for the sake of my moral improvement. My moral experience has such identifiable features, however I choose to respond to them.

My foundational evidence for God's reality and presence comes from the divine self-manifestation of God's perfectly good character and will in my experience. That evidence is experiential; it is not a belief or an argument. It has qualitative features of a morally relevant kind that I meet in my experience (see Gal. 5:22–24). It also goes against some of my familiar attitudes, tendencies, and actions. When this evidence is undefeated, relative to my total evidence, it can confer epistemic justification on my belief that God exists.

Going beyond the qualitative contents of my experience, I can reason and formulate arguments about my experiential evidence. I also can consider my belief that God exists to be central to a best available explanation of my overall experience. That belief is my best available answer to the following explanation-seeking question: Why am I having my present experience of moral dissonance rather than some other experience or no experience at all? A role for God's moral intervention figures in the best available explanation for my overall evidence. Even so, my foundational evidence of God's reality is experiential, and not a belief or an argument (see Moser [2018: chapter 5] and [2020: chapter 7 and 8]). A relevant explanatory argument can aid in presenting my evidence to other people, but such presenting is not to be confused with my having the relevant evidence.

With perfect redemptive caring, God would seek, at God's preferred time, to frustrate and subject to futility anything contrary to intended divine guidance, including wayward human aims. Paul thus remarks, as noted: "The creation was subjected to futility, not of its own will but by the will of the one who subjected it" (Rom. 8:20). The divine subjection of creation to futility would include the subjecting of an opposing human will to frustration and futility when God deems suitable.

God would use dissonance from goodness in moral experience, including in conscience, to challenge human wills opposed to God's will. The challenge would be toward their conformity with God's perfect moral character and will. So, the previous kind of moral dissonance from divine goodness in experience would have a divine purpose: the guidance of wayward humans toward (deeper) reconciliation with God. We need to clarify how such dissonance figures in divine guidance.

Integration from Dissonance

Dissonance in moral experience yields a conflict within people that threatens their moral integration or unity. It results in moral disintegration, at least for a time. A natural response to dissonance from God's intervening goodness comes from the prophet Isaiah: "Woe is me! I am lost, for I am a man of unclean lips, and I live among a people of unclean lips; yet my eyes have seen the King, the Lord of hosts!" (Isa. 6:5). A similar response came from the apostle Peter: "Simon Peter . . . fell down at Jesus's knees, saying, "Go away from me, Lord, for I am a sinful man!" (Luke 5:8). The pain of moral dissonance from divine goodness can prompt a desire for escape from the challenge.

An escape can come either from ignoring or rejecting the moral challenge from God or from agreeably cooperating with it. As long as the challenge persists, I will suffer a kind of moral disintegration. I will have an unresolved moral conflict in my moral experience and conscience that hinders the unity or integration of my moral life. I then will face moral division within my life. It will threaten my acting as a consistent moral agent, by nudging me in opposing directions.

I have two main options available for my free decision: On the one hand, I can ignore or reject God's better will, and, on the other hand, I can cooperate with it. Either option would remove the dissonance, at least from my awareness for a time. If I ignore or reject God's better will for the sake of my inferior will, I choose the moral low road. I then will persist, for instance, in my intention to steal from my neighbor, and my moral life will tend to go from bad to worse. This will be a moral life at odds with God, even if I have silenced my conscience, at least for a time, by ignoring or rejecting God's better will. This is an ongoing risk for moral agents inclined to choose their own ways over God's better will. To our detriment, we can suppress the divine moral attraction of goodness, even when God is at work in conscience.

We have the option to refuse cooperating with God's moral will and thus to refuse entering God's moral world as willing participants. A simple analogy may help. On the doorstep of a beautiful cathedral, we can choose not to enter but to view its stained-glass windows only from outside. We then see only dark shades on the windows, from their dark protective coverings, but we do not see the bright colors seen by viewers inside the cathedral. We then miss out on the attractive power of the beautiful windows, because we have not put ourselves in a position to apprehend their attractive power in its colorful fruition under better conditions.

Our choosing to enter the cathedral can make a big visual difference for us, given improved conditions for viewing. It can bring us acquaintance with the aesthetic power of the windows' colorful beauty under the better conditions. Our entering the cathedral is analogous to our entering God's moral world by cooperating with God's will. Using moral dissonance from experienced divine goodness, God invites people to enter the moral cathedral with appreciation of the beauty within. It is then their moral move, as free agents, to accept the invitation or not to accept it, that is, to cooperate or not to cooperate with God. Divine coercion of humans is not a live option here, because human agency is preserved by God for this decision. People can choose to stay outside the cathedral, in relative deprivation. In doing so, they can seek to integrate their moral lives without divine involvement. God, however, may have other desires for their lives.

Entering God's moral world, with due cooperation, brings integration to our moral lives around experienced divine goodness. It puts God's will first in our lives, and it takes us beyond the dissonance that threatens to leave us with moral disintegration. Our cooperation, however, need not be perfect; it is enough for a start that it be cooperative on balance in directing our lives toward God's will. The ideal is perfect cooperation, but this ideal need not be realized now for our cooperation on balance. The perfect does not exclude the good in the case of imperfect humans.

For now, we may assume, my overarching decision is to cooperate with God's will, including a commitment to follow through in particular cases. My decision leaves me struggling against my initial intention to steal from my neighbor, and it contributes to my deciding finally not to steal from him. God's moral will is thus realized in my cooperation. I have entered God's moral world as a willing participant, and it differs from my self-defined moral world. It has an interpersonal feature that gives me profoundly good moral challenges, beyond the challenges from myself and other humans. It also brings moral depth and improvement to my moral life.

Paul thought of divine guidance in the midst of dissonance as follows: "It is God who is at work in you, enabling you both to will and to work for his good pleasure" (Phil. 2:13). He acknowledged the importance of God's enabling, but not coercing, people to will in a certain way. The divine enabling involves an experience of God's moral character and will of righteous love as evidence that sets a moral standard for a person: "Hope [in God] does not disappoint us, because God's love has been poured into our hearts through the Holy Spirit that has been given to us" (Rom. 5:5). This love is a divine self-manifestation of God's moral character and love, and Paul thought of it as not only experienced but also motivating for a person. He thus remarks: "The love of Christ urges us on," on the assumption that this is *God's* love *from* Christ (2 Cor. 5:14). This kind of divine motivating guidance toward cooperative people figures in his aforementioned understanding of being a child of God: "All who are led by the Spirit of God are children of God" (Rom. 8:14).

Being led by God includes being attracted by God's perfect goodness to cooperate with God's will self-manifested in experience. This kind of being led guides a person, without coercion, to conform to God's moral character in (deeper) reconciliation with God. In being thus led, a human moral character is integrated with divine goodness, thereby bringing unity to moral experience and conscience. It also receives experiential evidence of God's presence in a human life, while undergoing moral renewal in conjunction with human cooperation with God. The evidential and the moral domains work together in a transformative manner as humans cooperate with divine guidance.

A significant transformation occurs in human moral character, given cooperation with divine guidance, and this bears on human evidence of God's reality. Rufus Jones has remarked:

> The monumental evidence of God is ... the fact of spiritual personality through which divine traits of character are revealed. Stars and mountains and ordered processes of nature reveal law and mathematics and beauty, but they reveal and can reveal no traits of character, no qualities of personality, no warmth and intimacy of heart and mind. If we are ever to be convinced that self-giving love is a reality of God's nature, we shall be convinced by seeing this love break through some human organ of [God's] Spirit. (1931: 217)

Human-personality transformation toward God's character or personality arises from divine guidance as a human cooperates with the self-manifestation of God's morally perfect will in experience. Such transformation is a central goal of divine guidance, for the sake of righteousness among humans.

Viewed from the inside perspective of cooperating with God's will, the transformation can give one firsthand experiential evidence of divine reality and guidance. Viewed from the outside perspective without cooperating with God, the evidence will tend to be ambiguous at best for a person, given an absence of firsthand experience of divine leading. So, we should not expect the relevant evidence from divine guidance to be universally compelling. This is the result of its interpersonal volitional nature, coupled with volitional variation among humans.

Divine character transformation of a human goes beyond the following of moral rules to the interpersonal acquaintance and cooperation of a human with God as self-presented in moral experience. Morality takes on new depth and power in this interpersonal perspective, courtesy of God's morally empowering role in moral experience. This newness will be apprehended by people inside, who join in cooperation with God. They will be akin to the people who see the bright colors of the stained-glass windows from inside the cathedral. They will have an evidential and moral perspective of divine power and guidance unknown to people who choose to remain outside. They will know the morally powerful leading of God firsthand, while people outside will not.

The divine guidance is not human self-leading, because the moral depth of the guidance is not resident in typical humans. This becomes clear, and the plot thickens, once we acknowledge that the divine leading moves in a direction atypical for humans: toward love of enemies as willing what is good for them. Jesus, as indicated, was clear about this demanding direction God takes, in keeping with God's perfect moral character:

> You have heard that it was said, "You shall love your neighbor and hate your enemy." But I say to you, Love your enemies and pray for those who persecute you, so that you may be children of your Father in heaven; for he makes his sun rise on the evil and on the good, and sends rain on the righteous and on the unrighteous. For if you love those who love you, what reward do you have? Do not even the tax collectors do the same? And if you greet only your brothers and sisters, what more are you doing than others? Do not even the Gentiles do the same? Be perfect, therefore, as your heavenly Father is perfect. (Matt. 5:43–48; cf. Luke 6:32–36)

According to Jesus, we must cooperate with God's guiding us to love of our enemies if we are to be children of God. He anchored this demand in God's moral perfection, and he offered no exceptions to the scope of divine love's demand. (For historical background, see Meier [2009: 499–527].)

Jesus used the parable of the prodigal son to illustrate God's quest for divine–human reconciliation even for people opposed to God's perfectly loving ways (Luke 15:11–32). (See Moser [2021b: chapter 5].) He also manifested the love in question with his befriending and eating with social outcasts of questionable moral standing. He expected the same of his followers (Matt. 25:34–45). So, entering God's moral world with due cooperation may be integrating with divine goodness, but it is not easy or casual for typical humans. Given wayward human moral tendencies, we should not expect acquaintance or cooperation with a God of perfect goodness to be easy or casual. Instead, we should expect a struggle with dissonance for the sake of realizing divine goodness in our lives. We turn to the bearing of evil on divine guidance.

Guiding through Evil

Divine guidance toward righteousness meets resistance from evil in the world. We should consider how such guidance proceeds in the face of evil, often without removing it. Some inquirers have asked whether divine failure to eliminate or to reduce actual human evil and suffering disqualifies God from being worthy of worship and trust. We thus should ask whether God can escape a charge of divine neglect for human evil and suffering.

We should consider the adequacy of a vantage point from which divine goodness and guidance are assessed. If a human vantage point is so narrow as to be misleading regarding divine goodness and guidance, it can be inferior to other available vantage points. Our attention to this consideration will suggest a widely neglected vantage point of a *showing-how theodicy* that does not yield a comprehensive *explaining-why theodicy* regarding evil. The former theodicy includes God's using current evil and suffering to show, particularly in the lives of faithful people, how God will ultimately redeem and overcome all evil and suffering in God's preferred time. This approach fits with many of the Biblical narratives, and it enables God to sidestep a charge of divine inadequacy toward guidance in the face of human suffering. (For an earlier statement of a showing-how theodicy, see Moser [2022b].)

Many people hold that God's reality, goodness, and guidance are dubious at best because our evidence fails to indicate God's doing God's best to stop evil in the world. They suggest that even if an alleged "God" exists, that "God" would not be truly good and hence would not be truly God. The "God" in question, they propose, would not be worthy of our worship or trust. Some people report their having trusted God but becoming overwhelmed by the lack of helpful divine intervention in much human evil and suffering. They thus renounce the worthiness of God to be worshipped or trusted. So, we need to consider how God justifiably could allow and use human evil and suffering for good, without explaining for humans the full divine purpose in allowing them in some cases.

Good and Bad Suffering

We may use the terms "suffering" and "pain" interchangeably to connote human distress of a kind that typically prompts a human adjustment for intended avoidance. The OED offers:

Pain –   Unpleasant or agonizing physical sensation ... . The state or condition of consciousness arising from mental or physical suffering .... Mental distress or suffering; anguish, grief.

Suffering – The bearing or undergoing of pain, distress, or tribulation.

Distress is a central factor, but we should acknowledge that suffering typically includes an intention to avoid its distress. Humans rarely desire the distress of their suffering, and they usually desire not to have it at all.

We can consider some human suffering to be good on the basis of its good direct effects. The suffering in my daily exercise, for instance, illustrates this when it has only good direct effects, such as improving my muscles. We can extend this lesson to moral goodness in the case of some suffering (if in combination with human selfishness) that has only morally good direct effects. We also can consider some suffering to be good on the direct basis of a successful intention to make the suffering good. For instance, I can successfully intend my suffering in my daily exercise to strengthen my back muscles and thereby to save me from worse back pain. In addition, we can assess a case of suffering by its inherent felt quality, such as the felt quality of receiving unselfish care from a person. This can be a good experience, even a morally good experience, on the basis of its felt quality. It would be a mistake, then, to hold that every experience of human suffering is inherently bad or even morally bad.

Many people hold that God does not cause human suffering. Their ground is often that human suffering is inherently bad and God would not cause what is inherently bad. This position, however, contradicts the central Biblical portrait of God as an agitator for righteousness among humans even by means of bringing about their suffering. It also contradicts the New Testament portrait of Jesus as God's supreme representative who often brought the distress of suffering to his audience. For instance, the four New Testament Gospels portray Jesus as overturning the tables of the money-changers in the temple and driving the money-changers out (Mark 11:15–19, Matt. 21:12–17, Luke 19:45–48, John 2:13–16). Jesus also raised many distressful challenges to his disciples and other inquirers, particularly in his representing what God expects of them. For instance, the response of the inquiring rich man to Jesus was: "When he heard this, he was shocked and went away grieving" (Mark 10:22; cf. Matt. 19:22). A discussion of God and suffering, then, should clarify what kind of God is at issue, in relation to a divine role in human suffering.

God for Good Suffering

Human denial of the worthiness of God to be trusted or even considered to be real is typically too quick. A big question is: Trusted or considered *for what*? What, in particular, should people expect God to be trustworthy *for*? One might reply: For what *I* (or we) deem to be good, to be given to *me* (or us) when *I* (or we) want it. This reply differs from a significant alternative: We should expect God to be trustworthy for what *God* deems to be good, to be given when *God* desires.

A factor in favor of the latter alternative is that God, as perfectly good, would be in a better position than typical humans to decide the matter. Cognitive modesty for humans recommends as much. This fits with Paul's blunt response: "It is God who justifies. Who is to condemn? It is Christ Jesus, who died ... " (Rom. 8:33–34).

God would have a vantage point, beyond human vantage points, for bringing about good for the long term rather than just the short term. God's vantage point thus can leave humans with mystery about many divine purposes, particularly in God's allowing evil and suffering. In addition, a human perspective considering just the short term could leave us with a missed opportunity for realizing what is good over the long term, including for a maximal number of people. This factor can yield a reason to wait patiently, if with some mystery, for good in God's time rather than just in the short term. God may decide to postpone making the short term fully good for the sake of more enduring and inclusive good in the long term. God's bringing about full goodness thus can be future-oriented and hence eschatological, in the fullness of time. We humans, in any case, are in no position to exclude this option.

Section 1 indicated that the Biblical God, without causing evil, actively agitates for what is good and does not simply wait for it. As a result, this God creates stumbling blocks for people as challenging occasions for their moral offense, in order to attract them to what is genuinely good in relation to God and others. So, divine guidance works with moral stumbling blocks as challenges aiming at human improvement in relation to God.

According to the book of Isaiah, God is a stumbling block, and not just a sanctuary, to humans for the sake of their righteousness:

> The Lord of hosts, him you shall regard as holy; let him be your fear, and let him be your dread. He will become a sanctuary, a stone one strikes against; for both houses of Israel he will become a rock one stumbles over – a trap and a snare for the inhabitants of Jerusalem. And many among them shall stumble; they shall fall and be broken; they shall be snared and taken. (Isa. 8:13–15)

Divine "holiness" includes divine righteousness as robust moral goodness set on overcoming evil, and God agitates for it among humans. Unlike the gods of deism or mere theism, this is a God of disturbing moral goodness who disturbs humans, even with suffering, in order to guide them to moral and spiritual goodness in relation to God.

The book of Jeremiah announces a God who sets painful stumbling blocks to promote righteousness, sometimes with judgement: "Hear, O earth; I am going to bring disaster on this people, the fruit of their schemes, because they have not given heed to my words; and as for my teaching, they have rejected it .... Therefore, thus says the Lord: See, I am laying before this people stumbling blocks against which they shall stumble; parents and children together, neighbor and friend shall perish" (Jer. 6:19, 21; cf. Ezek. 3:20). A God who sets such stumbling blocks gets an inadequate hearing from contemporary writers on theodicy. Many people now dismiss the reality of God on the ground that evidence for God is absent from human experience. The God of Isaiah and Jeremiah, however, is known for setting distressful moral challenges in the experience, and thus the evidence, of wayward humans. These challenges are for the sake of divine guidance of humans toward righteousness.

Paul, we noted, acknowledged God's agitating for righteousness in the everyday lives of humans, including in subjecting the anti-God world to futility (Rom. 8:20–21). God, however, does not leave people with a full explanation of the divine purposes for setting stumbling blocks or for allowing evil and suffering in the world. So, God does not take full human understanding of God's specific purposes to be required by what is valuable for humans now. As a result, we should not expect to have a full explanatory theodicy now of God's purposes toward humans. We have a ground for expecting not to have such a theodicy.

Paul cites the book of Isaiah to confirm that God undermines "human wisdom" of a certain kind:

> It is written, "I will destroy the wisdom of the wise, and the discernment of the discerning I will thwart." Where is the one who is wise? Where is the scribe? Where is the debater of this age? Has not God made foolish the wisdom of the world? For since, in the wisdom of God, the world did not know God through wisdom, God decided, through the foolishness of our proclamation, to save those who believe. For Jews demand signs and Greeks desire wisdom, but we proclaim Christ crucified, a stumbling block to Jews and foolishness to Gentiles, but to those who are the called, both Jews and Greeks, Christ the power of God and the wisdom of God. For God's foolishness is wiser than human wisdom, and God's weakness is stronger than human strength.
>
> (1 Cor. 1:19–25; cf. Isa. 29:14)

God, according to Paul, is not known through "human wisdom." Instead, God is known climactically through God's primary stumbling block for humans, Christ crucified, and Paul has in mind the risen, living Christ who was crucified. The latter knowledge relies on divine self-communication to humans, with the aid of a proclamation based on a unique divine intervention in human history and experience. This self-sacrificial intervention includes Christ crucified as God's supreme representative and sacrifice for reconciling humans to God (Rom. 3:24–25; cf. Heb. 2:17). (See Moser [2022a].)

Paul identifies God's purpose in divine self-communication that undermines "human wisdom": "God chose what is foolish in the world to shame the wise; God chose what is weak in the world to shame the strong; God chose what is low and despised in the world, things that are not, to reduce to nothing things that are, so that no one might boast in the presence of God" (1 Cor. 1:27–29). Humans tend to take self-credit for goodness to their own detriment, even when such credit is theirs to take. God uses an antidote to that harmful distortion, according to Paul, because the distortion enables humans to obscure who God is, especially in relation to them. It thus alienates them from God, including from a good opportunity for them in relating to God through divine goodness and guidance.

Paul, we have noted, specifies part of the divine antidote to harmful human wisdom: "My speech and my proclamation were not with plausible words of wisdom, but with a demonstration of the Spirit and of power, so that your faith might rest not on human wisdom but on the power of God" (1 Cor. 2:4–5). If humans are to trust and hope in God responsibly, and to be guided by God reliably, they will need a suitable ground or basis of evidence for their trust, hope, and being guided. Otherwise, a kind of arbitrariness will mark their relating to God, leaving them vulnerable to a charge of mere wishful thinking or otherwise being irrational from the standpoint of needed evidence. Paul counters by recommending that faith in God "rest on ... the power of God." That power is not just talk or theory. It is the main source and indication of divine self-manifestation in goodness to receptive, cooperative humans. It includes God's perfectly good love self-manifested to willing recipients in their experience at God's preferred times. It can emerge in their moral experience, including in their conscience, when they can benefit from it, such as when they are challenged to choose unselfish love for others.

If some people are not ready to cooperate with manifested divine love, God can withhold its manifestation to them while waiting for an opportune time. People sometimes are not ready to handle a divine intervention with due care and cooperation. So, God can show patience instead of evidential promiscuity or fanfare, sometimes hiding from people who would bring only harm out of divine self-manifestation to them (see Moser [2021c]). God, in any case, would not be a coercive bully or stalker toward humans in seeking to give divine guidance.

Paul does not reject wisdom altogether:

> Among the mature we do speak wisdom, though it is not a wisdom of this age
> or of the rulers of this age, who are doomed to perish. But we speak God's

wisdom, secret and hidden, which God decreed before the ages for our glory. None of the rulers of this age understood this; for if they had, they would not have crucified the Lord of glory. But, as it is written, "What no eye has seen, nor ear heard, nor the human heart conceived, what God has prepared for those who love him." (1 Cor. 2:6–9)

God's wisdom, according to Paul, differs from human wisdom in ways that create a stumbling block for humans, because it often eludes their expectation, prediction, and control. It also delivers a severe moral challenge to destructive human ways that alienate people from God. In addition, it postpones full goodness in the present or short term for a future prepared by God for its realization, even though divine goodness is revealed in part now to cooperative recipients (Rom. 8:18; cf. Matt. 19:28–29). We are in no position to fault God on moral grounds for that option.

Bounded Understanding

Paul represents the divine guidance of Abraham to proceed with "hoping against hope":

Hoping against hope, [Abraham] believed [παρ' ἐλπίδα ἐπ' ἐλπίδι ἐπίστευσεν] that he would become "the father of many nations," according to what was said, "So numerous shall your descendants be." He did not weaken in faith when he considered his own body, which was already as good as dead (for he was about a hundred years old), or when he considered the barrenness of Sarah's womb. No distrust made him waver concerning the promise of God, but he grew strong in his faith as he gave glory to God.

(Rom. 4:18–20; cf. Gen. 17:3–7)

Abraham is not hoping against *all* hope; that would be inconsistent. He is hoping against what any hope just from this world provides, independent of hope in *God and what God promises.*

God's promise to Abraham, in Paul's perspective, separates two kinds of hope: hope just from this world and hope from God. This prompts a natural human response: "Sarah laughed" (Gen. 18:12). The divine aim is to attract grounded human hope *in God,* rather than in anything independent of God and God's offering, including God's promise of redemption for humans. God can use the world to build hope in God, but that does not recommend hope in just what the world provides.

The divine redemptive challenge to humans includes a divide between human *understanding* of God's particular purposes in allowing evil and suffering and human trust or hope in *God.* The book of Job gives the classic illustration:

Job answered the Lord: "I know that you can do all things, and that no purpose of yours can be thwarted. 'Who is this that hides counsel without knowledge?' Therefore I have uttered what I did not understand, things too wonderful for me, which I did not know." "Hear, and I will speak; I will question you, and you declare to me." "I had heard of you by the hearing of the ear, but now my eye sees you; therefore I despise myself, and repent in dust and ashes." (Job 42:1–6)

Job's attitude fits with this proverb: "Trust in the Lord with all your heart and lean not on your own understanding" (Proverbs 3:5). It also receives support from the book of Jeremiah: "Thus says the Lord: Do not let the wise boast in their wisdom, do not let the mighty boast in their might, do not let the wealthy boast in their wealth; but let those who boast boast in this, that they understand and know me, that I am the Lord; I act with steadfast love, justice, and righteousness in the earth, for in these things I delight, says the Lord" (Jer. 9:23–24). Understanding "the Lord," in Jeremiah's perspective, does not require understanding why God allows all of this world's evils. Instead, it includes awareness that God stands for "love, justice, and righteousness in the earth," even if their full realization is postponed until God's fullness of time. Understanding *who God is*, then, can leave us with unanswered questions about many of God's purposes, and that should be no surprise for limited humans.

The divine redemptive aim for guidance is formed by *whom* God wants people ultimately to hope or trust in: namely, God. As the unique ultimate source of lasting good and meaning for human life, God would seek human hope and trust in that divine source, without those being diminished by other hopes and trusts. God thus would seek to clarify for humans the important difference between hope or trust in God and hope or trust in something at odds with God.

Humans must have some understanding of who God is to have suitably grounded and guided hope or trust in God, but full understanding is neither required nor available for them. Bounded understanding for humans is adequate, given divine purposes. God has a good purpose in blocking humans, as in the cases of Job and Abraham, from fully understanding God's aim in allowing evil and suffering. Even so, we can understand this larger purpose in general, without understanding many subsidiary purposes. God seeks to clarify for humans how hope and trust in God differ from hope and trust in human understanding of God's purposes. God's redemptive power is not in human understanding of God's purposes; it is in *God*, approached by trust and hope. Similarly, God can guide and save people toward lasting good life, but human understanding of God's purposes cannot do so. Our understanding is thus inferior to God's power in guidance.

We easily confuse hope and trust in God with hope and trust in something that seems close but is actually off the mark. We miss the mark with commitments that demote God, such as distorting God with a theology at odds with a perfectly righteous God. It is easy, for instance, for humans to hope and trust in divine benefits rather than in God. In that case, humans miss out on what really matters, the enduring source of the desired benefits. Divine stumbling blocks aim to challenge that tendency, in order to let God be God among humans and to leave room for humans to relate to God rather than to a counterfeit.

Some people object that God's stumbling blocks for humans are too harsh for a good God. They create too much human distress, so the objection goes, and they thus disqualify "God" from being a God worthy of worship and trust. There is, however, a complication if we assess just from our short-term perspective, apart from God's vantage point of future reparations. The objection suffers from an inadequate scope of evidence. It is questionable whether the objection applies from God's wider and longer vantage point, and we have noted the suggestion of Jesus and Paul that it does not apply. We would not be in a position, in any case, to fault God's better vantage point, because we lack access to its details for the future. Admitting a shortcoming in our evidence would thus be more defensible than alleging moral failure or indifference on God's part.

From God's perspective, wayward humans have a vital need to submit to God's goodness, for the sake of lasting good life. God would seek to show that need to humans for their benefit, sometimes through suffering. Human suffering can be a source of learning important needs and priorities for humans. A pressing question, however, concerns *how much* suffering and evil and *what severity* of suffering and evil God should allow in order to show humans their vital need of God. God, it seems, would be in a better position than humans to decide this matter. If so, we would not be in a position to exclude God's reality or goodness on the basis of this matter, given God's superior vantage point. We thus should acknowledge that the good ends of a truly good God can justify the means used by that God for good, even if those means include human suffering. God's goodness, however, would block any use of such a position to conclude that "anything goes" for God. (On divine teleology in a theodicy, see Forsyth [1916: chapter 7] and Leow [2011: chapter 4].)

Guiding for Theodicy Incarnate

God's unique vantage point underwrites the aforementioned distinction between a *showing-how* theodicy and a comprehenisve *explaining-why* theodicy. God can show how evil is or will be overcome, at least in general, for cooperative humans without fully explaining why God either brings about certain cases of human suffering or allows all cases of human suffering. It is question-begging, and a harmful mistake, to presume that God must justify divine ways by a full explaining-why theodicy rather than by a showing-how theodicy that manifests with righteousness how God will overcome evil, in God's good time. God has no moral obligation to block all evil now or to give us a full explanation of why God does not do so. Theology, like science, offers no full explanation of its domain.

The author of the Epistle to the Hebrews points to the basis of a showing-how theodicy in relation to Jesus as God's supreme representative and Son (Heb. 1:2–4):

> In subjecting all things to [humans], God left nothing outside their control. As it is, we do not yet see everything in subjection to them, but we do see Jesus, who for a little while was made lower than the angels, now crowned with glory and honor because of the suffering of death, so that by the grace of God he might taste death for everyone. It was fitting that God, for whom and through whom all things exist, in bringing many children to glory, should make the pioneer of their salvation perfect through sufferings . . . . Because he himself was tested by what he suffered, he is able to help those who are being tested. (Heb. 2: 8–10, 18)

The key claim is that, as human evil and suffering continue, "we do not yet see everything in subjection to humans, but we do see Jesus." We do not see everything in agreement with righteous goals, but we have Jesus to represent God's righteous response to evil and suffering. Jesus is the model for how God approaches human evil and suffering, and our approach to theodicy and divine guidance should accommodate this lesson.

Jesus is the supreme human case of God's theodicy incarnate, and he is a showing-how theodicy rather than a full explaining-why theodicy. The latter distinction is confirmed in Jesus's cry of dereliction on Calvary: "At three o'clock Jesus cried out with a loud voice, 'Eloi, Eloi, lema sabachthani?' which means, 'My God, my God, why have you forsaken me?'" (Mark 14:34; cf. Matt. 27:46). Jesus does not get or give a full answer to his explanation-seeking question, even if it seems that God owes him an explanatory answer. Instead, Jesus shows with his own life how God responds to unjust suffering, by self-identifying with sufferers without giving an adequate explanation of their suffering. In doing so, he presents a model for the unjust suffering of other people. (On his felt abandonment by God, see Rossé [1987] and Bauckham [2008: 268].).

Jesus aims to show something distinctive of God: When God has people endure unjust suffering, while incarnating divine righteousness, their suffering is eventually redeemed in transformation toward God's greater righteousness, finally through resurrection. They typically do not fully or even adequately understand God's purposes in causing or allowing their suffering. Even so, they come to experience firsthand how God brings greater good out of their suffering, in God's good time, ultimately in their resurrection to new life with God. In Luke's Gospel, Jesus sidesteps an occasion to explain why suffering has occurred and focuses instead on a good human relationship to God, regardless of surrounding circumstances (Luke 13:3–4). He thus seeks to have people incarnate God's greater righteousness prior to, and even without, a full explaining-why theodicy. His followers are to do likewise.

The incarnation of righteousness sought through divine guidance is that of God's Spirit incarnate in a person, that is, the indwelling Spirit of Christ (Rom. 8:9–10). Such indwelling relies on the inward obedience of Gethsemane manifested by Jesus in the face of his predicted demise in Jerusalem. Jesus thus died to any contrary will of his own into his incarnating God's Spirit and will: "Not what I want, but what You [God] want" (Mark 14:36; cf. Phil. 2:8). This is Gethsemane guidance by God, and the people of God are expected to follow suit (Mark 8:34–36), thus incarnating and manifesting God's enduring righteousness, even when humans lack their own solutions and explanations for evil and suffering. So-called "natural evil" sets a fitting context for this divine challenge for being guided to theodicy incarnate; it, too, resists a full explanatory theodicy now for humans.

An available theodicy of God is not in the avoidance, the abolishment, or the full explanation of evil. It is, instead, in the continuance of God's manifested Spirit in the righteous sufferer who abides cooperatively with God, thereby showing divine righteousness without disowning God. (Psalm 71 anticipates what Jesus showed in this regard.) Jesus thus calls to "My God, my God," despite his unanswered why-question about felt abandonment by God. Inwardly and resolutely, he sides with God, and waits for divine rescue in resurrection. God's continuing with him toward greater righteousness, including when he feels abandoned, shows God's worthiness of worship and trust, even without a full explaining-why theodicy. The same applies to other people willing to incarnate a showing-how theodicy in the absence of full explanation and of current experience of divine presence. God thus is shown to be worthy of greater value and honor than full explanation of evil and even of current human experience of divine presence.

Jesus willingly died into his resurrection by God, but he relied on the firm ground of his previous experience of God's unmatched goodness as his father (see Moser [2021a: chapter 3]). As a result, he predicts his resurrection three times in Mark's Gospel, despite his impending deadly suffering (8:31–32, 9:31, 10:33–34). Likewise, as suggested, his followers have a foretaste of God's greater goodness that saves them from disappointment and despair (Rom 5:5).

Their hope in God, despite unexplained evil and suffering, has a ground in God's unique experiential intervention in the lives of the people of God.

God's children share in divine suffering as Jesus did, "always carrying in the body the death of Jesus, so that the life of Jesus may also be made visible in our bodies" (2 Cor. 4:10). They thereby incarnate the same Spirit that led Jesus into the wilderness, then to Gethsemane, and finally to Calvary, thus extending the theodicy incarnate in Jesus (cf. Col. 1:24). Paul therefore remarks: "We do not lose heart. Even though our outer nature is wasting away, our inner nature is being renewed day by day. For this slight momentary affliction is preparing us for an eternal weight of glory beyond all measure" (2 Cor. 4:16–17; cf. Rom. 8:18). Divine guidance toward such renewal is not to be had on the cheap. The life of Jesus makes this clear, if it makes anything clear.

Some people say, as noted, that the alleged divine allowance and guidance toward suffering are excessive for a good God. It is questionable, however, whether they are in a good position to say. A person's judgment regarding a showing-how theodicy will depend for its credibility on that person's actual evidence regarding God's goodness. That evidence can and does vary with human receptivity to cooperation with divine goodness. The relevant evidence can be hidden, either by God or by human moral blindness, as a result of human opposition or indifference toward God. So, if some people give God the benefit of the doubt, on the basis of their evidence, others will refuse to do so, on the basis of their evidence. This will and does leave us with diversity and even conflict in human beliefs about God's reality, goodness, and guidance.

The needed evidence of divine reality, goodness, and guidance comes via a major obstacle. Evidence of God's unique character includes evidence of divine self-sacrificial love for the good of others. God would expect humans to recipro-cate with the same kind of love toward God and others, even their harshest critics and enemies (Matt. 5:43–48, Luke 6:32–36, Rom. 12:1–2, 19–21). Trusting God would require such reciprocating when the opportunity arises. Similarly, appro-priating the distinctive evidence of God's character in its intended fruition would require cooperating with it, in terms of its moral expectations for humans. This would be a central part of being guided by God. Humans often pull back in fear of loss, and their evidence of God's distinctive power and guidance in righteous love thus dwindles. They then fail to share God's moral vantage point and miss out on God's intended theodicy incarnate. The result is human failure to allow for divine guidance. Our attitudes thus matter for our being well-positioned to receive evidence of divine goodness and guidance and thus evidence for a showing-how theodicy.

Our pulling back from divine guidance would not leave God in despair. As indicated, the book of Isaiah represents God as follows: "All day long I have held out my hands to an obstinate people, who walk in ways not good, pursuing their own imaginations" (Isa. 65:2; cf. Rom. 10:21). It remains for humans to respond, ideally without indifference, arrogance, or despair. A showing-how theodicy is at stake for humans, proceeding not by full explanation but by overcoming evil in due course with experienced divine renewal for good. Why, then, does God opt for guidance toward a lived showing-how theodicy rather than a full explaining-why theodicy? A concise answer: A showing-how theodicy better manifests God's unique character and values in a redemptive manner. Inquirers now can benefit by considering that divine vantage point for their own suffering and the evil they face. We turn to how divine guidance is to be assessed for authenticity from that vantage point.

4 Guided Cooperative Discernment

Test everything; hold fast to what is good. – 1 Thessalonians 5:21

Having portrayed divine guidance as based on God's distinctive moral charac-ter, we now can make sense of how such guidance can become a credible reality for receptive humans. The credibility, we shall see, depends on the attitudes of humans toward their cooperation with the guidance in question. We shall see why this is so and how it bears on human evidence for divine guidance.

Testing for a Guiding God

We have mentioned Paul's following conviction about divine guidance of the Christians at Philippi: "It is God who is at work in you, enabling you both to will and to work for his good pleasure" (Phil. 2:13). We can characterize and test for this guidance in the light of divine jealous righteousness operative in human experience. If we neglect such righteousness, we easily can overlook God's reality and guidance aiming to own humans as God's people responsible for righteousness. We then can fail to see God's jealous love for humans at work, if painfully, in their lives.

The book of Isaiah portrays God as inviting King Ahaz of Judah to test God by asking for a sign from God: "The Lord spoke to Ahaz, saying, 'Ask a sign of the Lord your God; let it be deep as Sheol or high as heaven'" (Isa. 7:10–11). If we are testing for God's reality or guidance, we should seek a sign of the reality of God's unique character, rather than something incidental about God. This will leave us with guidance in the absence of visual evidence of God, but it will fit God's distinctive character.

The Biblical God, as suggested, aims to guide humans via the moral frustra-tions and challenges that nudge them toward righteousness and away from selfishness and moral complacency. If those frustrations and challenges seem to be goal directed toward righteousness, they can be the results of an intentional God using frustration and futility to invite humans to righteousness in relation to God and God's kingdom. People thereby can be morally attracted by God to submit to divine righteousness, without being coerced.

As noted, we should not expect God to work by divine coercion of human wills. Human cooperation plays a key role, thus preserving genuine human agency and responsibility. Such agency and responsibility are assumed in the following portrait of God noted previously: "I held out my hands all day long to a rebellious people, who walk in a way that is not good, following their own devices" (Isa. 65:2; cf. Rom. 10:21). People have the autonomy to opt out of God's righteousness, as history confirms abundantly. So, humans have the power to frustrate God's redemptive goal and guidance for themselves. They thus can misuse their autonomy against divine guidance, often with tragic results.

Divine jealousy for righteousness, we have suggested, can be experienced in our moral challenges akin to Jesus's moral struggle with God in Gethsemane. Gethsemane included a moral struggle for Jesus between two wills, and humans in general can experience such a struggle in their own lives. Jesus initially balked at God's will, requesting: "Remove this cup from me" (Mark 14:36). He moved, however, to resolute cooperation with God's challenge to sacrifice his life for God's kingdom: "Yet, not what I want, but what you want" (Mark 14:36).

Jesus's cooperative response came via painful struggle with God's demanding will: "He . . . began to be distressed and agitated. And he said to them [Peter, James, and John], 'I am deeply grieved, even to death'" (Mark 14:33–34). God used such painful struggle to guide Jesus to full alignment with God's will, for the promotion of divine righteousness among humans. This kind of experience manifests the reality of divine jealousy for the filial possession of humans, with the obedient Jesus as the filial model calling God "Abba, Father" (Mark 14:36) (see Moser [2021a: chapter 3]). Paul applies the same filial theme to the disciples of Jesus, with a similar role for calling God "Abba, Father" (Rom. 8:13–16) (see Moser [2022a]). Divine guidance is motivated by such filial jealousy.

Many theologians ignore the prominent theme of divine jealousy in the Jewish scriptures. Many thus write books on divine love in Judaism and Christianity without pursuing the theme at all (see Nygren [1953]; Outka [1972]; Morris [1981]; and Vacek [1994]). As a result, much theology loses sight of divine jealousy for righteousness. This omission often results in either an undue narrowing or an undue widening of the domain of divine action and guidance. Kant retreated to relevant divine work only in the moral law, thus neglecting divine activity in moral experience beyond the moral law (see Baillie [1939: chapters 4 and 5]). We find a different kind of undue narrowing in existential theologians influenced by Bultmann who limit relevant evidence to anthropological matters of understanding human existence. (For discussion, see Richardson [1964: 147–53].) At the other extreme, some theologians focus on cosmological or teleological considerations involving nature, to the exclusion of divine immanence in experienced jealousy for righteousness. Such a focus is found in much of traditional Christian apologetics relying on theistic arguments, such as those from Aquinas, that neglect God's direct convicting role in moral experience. The price paid is the neglect of the key evidential role of such divine jealousy in human moral lives, including in divine guidance.

Paul held that experienced divine goodness, including divine kindness, has a definite purpose aimed at righteousness. He thus asks, as indicated: "Do you despise the riches of [God's] goodness and forbearance and patience? Do you not realize that God's goodness is meant to lead you to repentance?" (Rom. 2:4). We have seen that experienced divine jealousy, however severe, has a similar goal: to lead people to a righteous relationship with God and thereby with other people. The experienced challenge via such jealousy is intended by God to indicate divine caring for righteousness in relationships, between God and humans, and between humans and humans. It thus serves as important evidence for God's reality and guidance, despite its being widely neglected.

When people cooperate with the divine challenge aimed at righteousness, we have suggested after Paul, they find a ground of assurance for their faith and hope in God: "Hope [in God] does not disappoint us, because God's love has been poured into our hearts through the Holy Spirit that has been given to us" (Rom. 5:5). The test for God's reality and presence is thus confirmed via God's unique self-presentation of divine *agapē* in the moral experiences of cooperative recipients. That *agapē,* we have seen, is jealous over divine righteousness, including over God's kingdom of God's children submitted to such righteousness. When people disregard God's righteous intervention, God can properly withdraw divine self-manifestation to enable them to see the ultimate futility of their lives apart from filial possession by God, including righteous reconciliation with God. This is one redemptive motive behind the phenomenon of divine hiding at times.

We now can see the importance of attentiveness to divine jealousy, as a feature of God's righteous character and guidance that can emerge in human moral experience. If part of a best explanation of our moral experience is that a jealous God is agitating for righteousness, we have an experiential basis for taking such a divine effort seriously, as a vital reality for our moral lives.

We then have a basis for considering seriously an alternative to ultimate futility in our lives, even if parts of our lives are subjected to futility by God. So, the reality of divine jealousy bears on the significance of our lives and on the nature of our moral experience and evidence regarding God and divine guidance.

Guiding toward Enemy Love

The Biblical God cannot be reduced to the solution of a merely intellectual problem for humans. Jeremiah indicates the moral robustness required for knowing and testing for this righteous God who seeks to rule and guide uncoercively but also to self-hide when appropriate:

> Did not your father eat and drink
> and do justice and righteousness?
> Then it was well with him.
> He judged the cause of the poor and needy;
> then it was well.
> Is not this to know me?
> says the Lord (Jer. 22:15–16).

This God thus aims to lead people to the *doing* of righteousness, beyond mere thinking and arguing about God and righteousness. (See Heschel [1962: 195–220].) Opting out of the doing of righteousness can result in God's withdrawing from one's awareness, including conscience and related moral experience, until an opportune time when one is prepared to cooperate in action. Human reflection is thus not the final goal for this God who seeks to lead humans in righteous action and life. (On the role of conscience and moral experience in evidence for divine reality, see Forsyth [1913] and Moser [2020: chapters 7 and 8].)

Willingly being led by divine righteousness is central to human knowing God aright, beyond mere knowledge that God exists. Jeremiah had in mind participatory knowing of God, including willingly sharing in and being led by God's righteousness, of the kind that can deliver human redemption by God. It goes beyond a mere intellectual response to evidence of God because it requires human volitional cooperation with that evidence as formative for a human life-direction. Participatory knowing thus can reorient a life toward sharing in and being led by God's distinctive moral life, including in enemy-love.

The relevant evidence of God's reality and guidance is not limited to intellectual factors, such as arguments. It includes experiential features that represent God's moral character and will, and those features can have attractive and thus motivational power for a willing person. The model for participatory knowing of God is set by Jesus in Gethsemane. In response to God's moral challenge for him, he puts God's will first, above his own, in a way that enables

God to empower and guide his life in obedient righteousness. His disciples are called to follow suit, obeying God as "Abba" (Mark 14:36–41), the father who cares for and guides them (see Moser [2018: chapter 3]).

Buber rightly objects to reducing the domain of God and divine guidance to the domain of ethical matters. He remarks that "the absolute norm [in the domain of ethics] is given [by God] to show the way that leads [humans] before the face of the Absolute [that is, God]" (1952: 105). How does this intended "leading" (or guiding) to the face of God proceed? The answer is central to how God can be an Über-King and Über-God who leads humans without relying on a human system of supervision and while relying on self-hiding from some people at times.

The key is in goal-directed divine goodness in human experience as the basis for intended divine leading. The divine power in such intended leading takes the initiative in human experience, with different kinds of good interruption in experience, but it seeks human cooperation, without the divine coercion of human wills toward God. We can respond in social groups, including with consultation from other people, but this does not allow for an individual response by proxy. Each person must be led, and respond, to God in Gethsemane, after the model set by Jesus.

Through human cooperation, God's righteous power of goodness comes to active fruition in a human life as the redemptive, rightening power it is intended to be. Without such cooperation, the presentation of such power is frustrated by human recalcitrance or complacency, and a person then may fail to see its unique power in its fruition. William Newton Clarke identifies what lies in the background here: "It is [ideal] that the flower advance to the fruit of which it is the promise, and the fruit is the character worthy of such a being. The character that is worthy of a human being is the lowly reproduction of the character of God" (1909: 104).

The divine self-hiding prompted by human resistance can save a person from doing further damage toward a righteous divine–human relationship on offer. It can provide an opportunity, and needed time, for one's later, more judicious reconsideration of a new life-direction toward righteousness. So, divine leading can be complicated; it can be postponed and even rejected by human attitudes and responses.

Humans have a morally sensitive test for the authenticity of divine leading. It becomes effective when their cooperation with divine righteousness in their experience empowers them actively to become more righteous and less unright-eous in ways exceeding mere human tendencies. A salient feature is the emergence of righteousness that includes love of one's enemies, even at one's own risk. Such love manifested in human experience is best explained as anchored in divine self-manifestation, and thus as an identifying feature of goal-directed divine goodness, from God. Paul thinks of God's love for us to precede our welcoming or otherwise responding to God, while we are ungodly enemies of God (Rom. 5:6, 10). God's goodness and love thus come to human enemies of God, who do not merit that goodness and love (cf. Rom. 4:2–4). If we inquirers about God fail to see that this consideration applies to us and not just to *our* enemies, we may fail to appreciate the scope and power of divine love, including what Paul calls "grace."

Before Paul, we have noted, Jesus represented God's enemy-love to be integral to God and to being children of God: "You have heard that it was said, 'You shall love your neighbor and hate your enemy.' But I say to you, Love your enemies and pray for those who persecute you, so that you may be children of your Father in heaven; for he makes his sun rise on the evil and on the good, and sends rain on the righteous and on the unrighteous" (Matt. 5:43–45; cf. Luke 6:35–36). According to Jesus, enemy-love is God's unique signature, and Paul agrees, in the wake of Jesus (Rom. 12:9–10, 20–21; cf. Rom. 5:6, 10).

Paul, as suggested, acknowledges God's unique love being poured by God's Spirit into the hearts of people receptive to it. This love includes uniquely divine enemy-love, distinguishing it from typical human love. Typical humans are not inclined to practice enemy-love or to support it, even on reflection. The same is true of many traditional claimants to the title "God." Jesus, however, portrayed God as distinctive in enemy-love, and we thus should be attentive to God's intervening Spirit to self-manifest divine love accordingly. In the absence of such love, we would have a case for agnosticism about a God worthy of worship.

Active divine guiding toward enemy-love among humans is no small matter; it brings the ring of truth to a claim to divine leading. We humans, when candid, have enough awareness of what righteousness requires to rely on such a test in many cases, even if we face some gray areas at times. We know, for instance, that the notorious abuses by ISIS are unrighteous, even if we lack a precise argument for what we know. Similarly, we know that care for refugees in desperate need is righteous and commendable (cf. Lev. 23:22, 25:35, Deut. 10:19, 14:28–29), even without a precise argument. So, we need to separate the wheat from the chaff in interpretations of divine guidance, and we can make some progress with due candor and discernment.

If one discerns a moral challenge from goal-directed righteousness in experience, in God's good time, the stage will be set for divine guidance. At that point, a person faces a vital decision: to cooperate or not to cooperate; to be led or not to be led into (deeper) righteousness. This decision would be ongoing and uncoerced, with indifference amounting to a decision against the righteousness on offer and thus against God and divine guidance. The human freedom involved here is striking, as its use can be tragic or enlivening. God would refrain from making the latter choice for humans, in order to preserve genuine personhood as responsible agency here. God thus would leave room for other genuine persons, whether they are for or against divine righteousness. Whether, however, they leave room for themselves in God's kingdom is ultimately up to them.

Leaving room for God, according to Paul, includes human openness to being led by God. He thus remarks, as noted, that "all who are led by the Spirit of God are children of God" (Rom. 8:14). This perspective on the children of God mattered to Paul, because it enables God to be the rightful God of Gentiles as well as Jews (Rom. 3:29), and it includes his understanding of God as "Abba" (Rom. 8:15–16; cf. Gal. 4:6–7). Divine leading can transcend national and ethnic boundaries, and we should expect it to do so if God seeks the common good for humans of all backgrounds.

We see appreciation of God's universal goal in parts of ancient Israel, particularly where the broad scope of divine righteousness is recognized. The original promise to Abraham (Gen. 12:1–3) lies behind this inclusive perspective, and it calls for the kind of direct divine leading acknowledged by Jesus and Paul. We do well, then, to attend to such leading if we are to sustain the morally important attitude behind Abraham's vital question: "Shall not the Judge of all the earth do what is just?" (Gen. 18:25). That attitude must not be confused, however, with a demand for a public theophany in divine leading.

Guidance beyond Public Theophany

A noteworthy feature of ancient Israel is the departure of its Über-King from the use of public theophany to guide people. The book of Exodus reports public theophanies to Moses and the Israelites in the wilderness and at Mount Sinai (e.g., Exodus 19:11, 18–20, 20:1, 22, 24:9–11), but this pattern narrowed and eventually disappeared after Moses. The contrast, for instance, with divine intervention for Elijah at Mount Carmel is striking.

Samuel Terrien remarks:

> The threefold repetition "And Yahweh was not in the wind," "And Yahweh was not in the earthquake," "And Yahweh was not in the fire," constitutes a repudiation of not only the mode of divine intervention on Mt. Carmel but also of the possibility that the Mosaic theophany on Mt. Horeb could occur again in later history. The era of the theophany is now closed, and its validity is consigned to the hoary glamour of distant ages (1978: 231–32).

This claim of closure is about *public* theophany, and the change is hard to dispute, at least in general. An account of divine guidance needs to accommodate this change.

The core of the change is in the divine use of public visual evidence in divine guidance. Richard Elliott Friedman has commented on the divine response to Elijah at Mount Carmel: "It is just one dramatic stage in a series of stages, spanning the entire Jewish Bible, through which God step-by-step removes the visible markers of His presence" (1995: 24). The approach to divine guidance offered here makes sense of this change. The key is in divine moral leading toward interpersonal righteousness that does not require visible markers from God but proceeds instead with moral attraction from God.

The departure from visible markers is understandable if God is a Spirit (and not a visible body) set on morally robust interpersonal relations between God and humans. Such relations do not require visible markers for their existence or proliferation. John's Gospel has Jesus hint at this idea in his remark to Thomas: "Have you believed because you have seen [ἑώρακάς] me? Blessed are those who have not seen [ἰδόντες] and yet have come to believe" (John 20:29; cf. Matt. 16:17). Paul remarks in a similar vein: "We look not at what can be seen [βλεπόμενα] but at what cannot be seen; for what can be seen is temporary, but what cannot be seen is eternal" (2 Cor. 4:16–18; cf. Rom. 8:24–25). Paul thus highlights the requirement of the things of God being "spiritually discerned [πνευματικῶς ἀνακρίνεται]" (1 Cor. 2:14), and this includes yielding, cooperatively, to God's Spirit in action. Visible markers can get our attention at times, but they also can distract us from the divine Spirit morally at work among us and within us. Their value is thus limited at best, including in public settings.

Divine guidance extends to how we discern our moral experience relative to God, with prevenient help from God's leading Spirit. The priority in such leading thus belongs to God as kingly leader, but successful leadership in human action depends on our cooperation as we appreciate and conform to divine goodness in our experience. God is unveiled to us as righteous Über-King in that interaction, even without a public theophany or a visible sign. This kingly God is thus revealed in interpersonal righteousness, while being veiled to those who are not ready for such morally challenging transformation in divine leading. Divine self-hiding from humans, we have suggested, is often a form of divine waiting for them, with the patience of divine love. Even if God is Über-King and thus Über-Ruler over humans, the status of being *Über* will be unfulfilled among humans as long as they resist or ignore the divine guidance in their experience toward (deeper) righteousness.

A pressing question, taking us beyond mere reflection, is: Are we humans *willing* to be led in righteousness, including enemy-love, by the Über-King of Israel? This question is a divinely intended consequence of divine self-veiling and self-unveiling before humans, and its answer does not depend on a public theophany or any other visible sign from God. An assessment of divine hiding should begin with such considerations, if the God of Abraham, Isaac, Jacob, Jesus, and Paul is to receive a candid hearing.

Gambit for Divine Guidance

God's gambit in guiding humans takes a risk of failure from recalcitrant people, and many people fall into the latter group, to their long-term detriment. God either could give up on guiding people or God could opt for causal control of humans instead of guidance of them by moral attraction. Neither option, however, would deliver a family of responsible agents cooperating with God. In either case, God's longstanding ideal for a voluntary family that forms a righteous commonwealth would fail. The promise to Abraham then would come to nought. Instead, God opts for partial success in redemptive guidance, by respecting human agency and thus the reality of other persons in the divine gambit. The partiality of the success results from uncooperative humans, and not from God's causal will. God's effort at redemptive guidance by moral attraction respects genuine agency in human response. Otherwise, the Biblical story of divine redemption and guidance would be a sham.

Jesus told the parable of the sower to respond to the mixed results of his preaching the goods news of God's arriving kingdom. Some results relevant now are:

> These are the ones [where the word from God is] sown on rocky ground: when they hear the word, they immediately receive it with joy. But they have no root, and endure only for a while; then, when trouble or persecution arises on account of the word, immediately they fall away. And others are those sown among the thorns: these are the ones who hear the word, but the cares of the world, and the lure of wealth, and the desire for other things come in and choke the word, and it yields nothing. And these are the ones [where the word from God is] sown on the good soil: they hear the word and accept [παραδέχονται] it and bear fruit, thirty and sixty and a hundredfold.
>
> (Mark 4:16–20)

Jesus suggests that candidates for divine guidance are to "accept" that guidance in order for it to come to fruition in divine righteousness.

Luke's Gospel puts God's desired positive response from humans as follows: "As for that in the good soil, these are the ones who, when they hear the word, hold it fast [κατέχουσιν] in an honest and good heart, and bear fruit with patient endurance" (Luke 8:15). In the absence of such cooperative acceptance and commitment, divine guidance falls on inhospitable soil and fails to reach its intended fruition. So, divine guidance does not work with a magic wand. It takes responsible human agency seriously, with definite expectations for cooperation, and this entails a divine risk of failure owing to inadequate human response.

Human cooperation with God's will enables discernment of divine reality and guidance. It enables the relevant evidence of divine power to reach its salient fruition intended by God. It thus empowers cooperating people to see the divine power for the kind of distinctive transformative power it actually is: namely, righteous power that moves a person, without coercion, to be conformed to Christ as God's unique representative and son. Paul thus speaks of God's "purpose" of having people, Gentiles as well as Jews, "conformed to the image of his Son, in order that he might be the firstborn within a large family" (Rom. 8:28–29). Divine guidance should be understood in the light of this redemptive purpose, complete with divine family-building across ethnic and racial boundaries.

The very idea of a divine risk in a redemptive gambit offends many inquirers. They assume that divine power makes such a risk pointless. This assumption, however, betrays a harmful misunderstanding of divine guidance, at odds with the main teachings of Jesus and Paul. Their teachings portray God to seek a conquest over human unrighteousness not by coercion but by human cooperation in co-creation of a righteous family. Human cooperation with God's will contributes to the divine creation of a righteous family, and it thus enables responsible human co-ownership in the formation of that family.

God's gambit for divine guidance among humans allows rather than precludes unrighteousness and bad suffering among humans. Despite the absence of a full explanatory theodicy for us, we may infer that God values a righteous victory over those evils instead of a less demanding righteousness that does not win a victory for righteousness in relationships. A relevant factor is that hard-won righteousness is typically more durable and deeply appreciated among humans than righteousness that comes without shared victory over evil. Human valuing of righteousness rarely, if ever, comes on the cheap.

Although divine guidance comes by grace, as a divine gift, it is not easily received by humans. Its righteousness, intended to attract us morally, is at odds with many of our familiar ways, including our tendencies to selfishness. So, we face God's gambit for guidance with mixed responses. At times, like the rich young man responding to Jesus (Mark 10:17–22), we turn away for our own cause, if with some sorrow. Divine guidance, then, leaves us with some hard choices over time. They stem from a basic choice: Will we cooperate whole-heartedly with the divine righteousness on offer in our moral experience, or will we opt out of cooperation?

Our question amounts to this issue raised by divine guidance: Will we cooperate wholeheartedly with God? We thus are left with our settling on an answer, ideally on the basis of our overall evidence and what we should value. The result will inform the kinds of people we are and thereby the kinds of societies we inhabit. So, divine guidance matters for us, as much as anything matters.

References

Bauckham, Richard (2008). God's Self-Identification with the Godforsaken. In Richard Bauckham, *Jesus and the God of Israel*, Grand Rapids, MI: Eerdmans, 254–68.

Bird, Michael F. (2006). *The Saving Righteousness of God*, Milton Keynes: Paternoster.

Brueggemann, Walter (2009). *An Unsettling God*, Minneapolis, MN: Fortress Press.

Buber, Martin (1952). *Eclipse of God*, New York: Harper & Row.

Buber, Martin (1967). *Kingship of God, 3d ed.*, trans. Richard Scheimann, New York: Harper & Row.

Clarke, William Newton (1909). *The Christian Doctrine of God*. Edinburgh: T&T Clark.

Coogan, Michael (2019). *God's Favorites*, Boston, MA: Beacon Press.

Dodd, C. H. (1920). *The Meaning of Paul for Today*, New York: Doran.

Dodd, C. H. (1970). *The Founder of Christianity*, New York: Macmillan.

Dunn, James D. G. (1998). *The Theology of Paul the Apostle*, Grand Rapids, MI: Eerdmans.

Dunn, James D. G. (2003). *Jesus Remembered: Christianity in the Making, vol. 1*, Grand Rapids, MI: Eerdmans.

Eichrodt, Walther (1961). *Theology of the Old Testament*, vol. 1, trans. J. A. Baker, London: SCM Press.

Fitzmyer, Joseph A. (1981). *The Gospel according to Luke*, 2 vols., New York: Doubleday.

Forsyth, P. T. (1913). *The Principle of Authority*, London: Hodder & Stoughton.

Forsyth, P. T. (1916). *The Justification of God*, London: Duckworth.

Fretheim, Terence (1991). *Exodus*, Philadelphia, PA: Westminster Press.

Fretheim, Terence (2005). *God and World in the Old Testament*, Nashville, TN: Abingdon Press.

Friedman, Richard Elliott (1995). *The Disappearance of God*, Boston: Little, Brown.

Heschel, Abraham Joshua (1962). *The Prophets*, New York: Harper & Row.

Hultgren, Arland J. (1985). *Paul's Gospel and Mission*, Philadelphia, PA: Fortress.

Jeremias, Joachim (1967). *The Prayers of Jesus*, trans. John Bowden, et al. London: SCM Press.

Jillions, John A. (2020). *Divine Guidance*, New York: Oxford University Press.

Jones, Rufus (1931). *Pathways to the Reality of God*, New York: Macmillan.

Kierkegaard, Søren (1843). *Fear and Trembling and Repetition*, eds. and trans. Howard V. Hong and Edna H. Hong, Princeton: Princeton University Press, 1983.

Knight, George A. F. (1959). *A Christian Theology of the Old Testament*, London: SCM Press.

Leow, Theng Huat (2011). *The Theodicy of Peter Taylor Forsyth*, Eugene, OR: Pickwick.

Levenson, Jon D. (2016). *The Love of God*, Princeton: Princeton University Press.

McEntire, Mark (2013). *Portraits of a Mature God*, Minneapolis, MN: Fortress Press.

Meier, John (2009). *A Marginal Jew, vol. 4: Law and Love*, New Haven, CT: Yale University Press.

Mencken, H. L. (1930). *Treatise on the Gods*, New York: Knopf.

Mettinger, Tryggve N. D. (1988). *In Search of God*, trans. F. H. Cryer, Philadelphia, PA: Fortress Press.

Mikva, Rachel S. (2020). *Dangerous Religious Ideas*, Boston, MA: Beacon Press.

Miller, Patrick D. (2009). *The Ten Commandments*, Philadelphia, PA: Westminster Press.

Moberly, R. W. L. (2020). *The God of the Old Testament*, Grand Rapids, MI: Baker Academic.

Morris, Leon (1981). *Testaments of Love: A Study of Love In the Bible*, Grand Rapids, MI: Eerdmans.

Moser, Paul K. (2018). *The God Relationship*, Cambridge: Cambridge University Press.

Moser, Paul K. (2020). *Understanding Religious Experience*, Cambridge: Cambridge University Press.

Moser, Paul K. (2021a). Experiential Dissonance and Divine Hiddenness. *Roczniki Filozofiozne (Annals of Philosophy)* 69, 29–42.

Moser, Paul K. (2021b). *The Divine Goodness of Jesus: Impact and Response*, Cambridge: Cambridge University Press.

Moser, Paul K. (2021c). God *De Re et De Dicto:* Kierkegaard, Faith, and Religious Diversity. *Scottish Journal of Theology* 74, 135–46.

Moser, Paul K. (2022a). *Paul's Gospel of Divine Self-Sacrifice: Righteous Reconciliation in Reciprocity*, Cambridge: Cambridge University Press.

Moser, Paul K. (2022b). Theodicy Incarnate: Divine Self-Justification. *Expository Times* 133, 192–200.

Nygren, Anders. (1953). *Agape and Eros*, trans. P. S. Watson, London: SPCK.

Outka, Gene H. (1972). *Agape*, New Haven, CT: Yale University Press.

Oxford English Dictionary, 3d ed., Oxford: Oxford University Press, 2010.

Pascal, Blaise (1658). *Pensées*, trans. A. J. Krailsheimer, London: Penguin Books, 1966.

Richardson, Alan (1964). *History, Sacred and Profane*, London: SCM Press.

Rossé, Gérard (1987). *The Cry of Jesus on the Cross*, trans. S. W. Arndt, New York: Paulist Press.

Sanders, E. P. (1983). *Paul, the Law, and the Jewish People*, Minneapolis, MN: Fortress Press.

Smith, Mark S. (2001). *The Origins of Biblical Monotheism*, New York: Oxford University Press.

Snaith, Norman (1944). *The Distinctive Ideas of the Old Testament*, London: Epworth Press.

Terrien, Samuel (1978). *The Elusive Presence*, New York: Harper & Row.

Timmins, Will N. (2017). *Romans 7 and Christian Identity*, Cambridge: Cambridge University Press.

Vacek, Edward C. (1994). *Love, Human and Divine*, Washington, DC: Georgetown University Press.

Whitehead, A. N. (1933). *Adventures of Ideas*, New York: Macmillan.

Williams, Sam K. (1980). The "Righteousness of God" in Romans. *Journal of Biblical Literature* 99, 241–90.

Cambridge Elements ☰

The Problems of God

Series Editor
Michael L. Peterson
Asbury Theological Seminary

Michael Peterson is Professor of Philosophy at Asbury Theological Seminary. He is the author of *God and Evil* (Routledge); *Monotheism, Suffering, and Evil* (Cambridge University Press); *With All Your Mind* (University of Notre Dame Press); *C. S. Lewis and the Christian Worldview* (Oxford University Press); *Evil and the Christian God* (Baker Book House); and *Philosophy of Education: Issues and Options* (Intervarsity Press). He is co-author of *Reason and Religious Belief* (Oxford University Press); *Science, Evolution, and Religion: A Debate about Atheism and Theism* (Oxford University Press); *and Biology, Religion, and Philosophy* (Cambridge University Press). He is editor of *The Problem of Evil: Selected Readings* (University of Notre Dame Press). He is co-editor of *Philosophy of Religion: Selected Readings* (Oxford University Press) and *Contemporary Debates in Philosophy of Religion* (Wiley-Blackwell). He served as General Editor of the Blackwell monograph series Exploring Philosophy of Religion and is founding Managing Editor of the journal *Faith and Philosophy*.

About the Series
This series explores problems related to God, such as the human quest for God or gods, contemplation of God, and critique and rejection of God. Concise, authoritative volumes in this series will reflect the methods of a variety of disciplines, including philosophy of religion, theology, religious studies, and sociology.

Cambridge Elements ≡

The Problems of God

Elements in the Series

Divine Guidance: Moral Attraction in Action
Paul K. Moser

A full series listing is available at: www.cambridge.org/EPOG